CHOSEN

CHOSEN

—

Gay Catholic priests
tell their stories

Elizabeth Stuart

GEOFFREY
CHAPMAN

Geoffrey Chapman
An imprint of Cassell Publishers Limited
Villiers House, 41/47 Strand, London WC2N 5JE
387 Park Avenue South, New York, NY 10016-8810

First published 1993

British Library Cataloguing-in-Publication Data
A catalogue record for this book is available from the British Library.

Library of Congress Cataloging-in-Publication Data
Available from the Library of Congress.

ISBN 0-225-66682-0

Front cover: print by Sheena Barnes
Author photograph by Kevin Kelland

Typeset by Book Setters International Ltd
Printed and bound in Great Britain by
Biddles Ltd, Guildford and King's Lynn

Contents

Preface   ix

Introduction   1

Testimonies

Father Brian   33

Father David   38

Father Mark   41

Father Simon   43

Thomas, a seminarian   49

Vernon, a seminarian   52

Will, a seminarian   55

'Not a helpful place': the gay man and the seminary   61

'Ill-informed, lacking in understanding and compassion' attitudes to the Church's teaching on homosexuality   71

Glad to be gay?   77

Celibacy and sexual activity   84

Seeking support   91

Undermining the pedestal: the joy and pain of gay priests   99

'You are not alone': advice to future gay priests   104

The way forward: recommendations   110

Appendix: the questionnaire   113

Bibliography   115

For all gay Catholic priests in Britain

Preface

People picking up this book expecting a gay version of *The Thorn Birds*, or a salacious and voyeuristic collection of confessions from depraved priests, will be sadly disappointed. The stories that are told in this book are of very ordinary men, living ordinary lives serving the Catholic Church. What makes them extraordinary and in some people's eyes disordered and dangerous is that they happen to be gay. Sex makes little appearance in this book but love and the joys and pains love bring are always present. In the last few years an increasing number of Roman Catholic priests have been joining the Lesbian and Gay Christian Movement (LGCM), a large ecumenical organization in Britain which affirms the goodness and God-given-ness of gay and lesbian sexuality. The Roman Catholic Caucus of that organization has become increasingly aware of the enormous burdens gay Catholic clergy have to bear. They are unrecognized by the Church which they serve, which regards homosexuality as sinful and dangerous to society. They often suffer isolation, fear, rejection and self-hatred because of their sexuality. And above all these men feel they have no voice in the Church which they serve, even though gay clergy make up a significant proportion of the Catholic priesthood and they have much to teach the Church about sexuality, love and priesthood. But they cannot speak out openly. Gay priests who have dared to do so in the United States have paid a high price for their bravery. LGCM endeavours to be a voice for the voiceless and so the Roman Catholic Caucus became anxious to provide gay priests and seminarians with a 'safe' opportunity to share their stories. That was how this book was born. It does not claim to be a scientific survey. It does not claim to represent the views of all gay priests in Britain. It simply offers the stories and reflections of a group of British gay priests and seminarians who vary from one another in age, location, background, theology, attitude to sexuality and experience but who seem to share much in common. Since the Church professes to be one body and 'if one member suffers, all suffer together with it' (1 Corinthians 12:26) all of us, from the Pope to the laity, have a duty to be concerned about our gay pastors and to listen to them with love.

I am aware that this issue is related to others — married priests, women priests, priests who have left the ministry, and homosexuality in general — but I have chosen to concentrate only on gay priests and their stories because they deserve attention in their own right and have yet to receive it from the Church or from the gay community.

Thanks are due to the men who took the risk of telling me their stories. All names and personal details have been changed. Quest, another organization for lesbian and gay Catholics, graciously circulated questionnaires to priest members. Jane Robson drew up the questionnaire and helped to collate the material with her usual skill. The following generously helped to fund the project, Stanley Szarwark, Herman Bommer, Gordon Brown, Peter McGovern, David Bourner, Jerry Walsh, Sir John Knill, Rowan Swan, Anthony Jones, Rodney Targett, A. M. Goldie, Gerard McKell, Richard Frost, Christoph Bange, Jane Ledgley, Harry Lord and many more who wished to remain anonymous.

I hope the priest working at a British seminary who rang and begged me not to pursue this project, because 'things are so much better now' for gay priests and a book such as this would only cause trouble, will read the book and understand why it had to be written.

Elizabeth Stuart

Introduction

Gay clergy: historical background

There have always been gay priests and members of religious orders and congregations in the Roman Catholic Church. This is a fact that was frequently recognized and commented upon by non-Christian observers of the Church during medieval times and a fact that was used against the Church of Rome by Protestant reformers in the sixteenth century. It has always been an open secret within parts of the Church itself. The historian John Boswell claims to have found ceremonies to celebrate and cement same-sex relationships between clerics within the Roman and Greek Orthodox Churches which date from the fifth century onwards. During the age of courtly love in the eleventh and twelfth centuries some of the finest love poetry was written by monks and nuns to people of the same sex. St Aelred of Rievaulx (1109–67) had a strong emotional and sexual orientation towards men. He had several sexual relationships before becoming a monk and continued to fall in love with men once he entered the monastery. Having taken a vow of celibacy Aelred eschewed sexual relationships but he continued to delight in the passionate feelings he felt and shared with others. He believed that his capacity to have these passionate friendships was a gift from God and revealed something of the nature of God's love to him. Indeed, he believed that Jesus himself had such a relationship — 'a heavenly marriage' with the beloved disciple mentioned in John's gospel and described as resting on Jesus' breast at the last supper. By allowing and encouraging such chaste but passionate relationships between his monks when he was an abbot Aelred broke a strong taboo on 'particular friendships' between celibates, a taboo which was based upon centuries of hatred and fear of the body and its desires (and which is not unknown in the twentieth-century Church). Aelred knew from personal experience that great joy could be engendered and God encountered in sexual relationships and so he was not too harsh on those monks who broke their vows and engaged in sexual activity (John Boswell, *Christianity, Social Tolerance and Homosexuality* [University of Chicago Press, 1980], pp. 243–66).

Every so often outraged reformers within the Church would attempt to purge the Church of homosexually oriented clergy. For example, in the eleventh century St Peter Damian wrote a lengthy work entitled *The Book of Gomorrah* which urged the Pope to expel homosexual men from their orders. He believed that homosexual clergy confessed to one another to avoid detection and that their presence was corrupting the Church. Leo IX, however, refused to act as requested and argued that only persistent violations of the rule of celibacy were to be punished harshly. Pope Leo represents a period in which homosexuality among the clergy was tolerated and sexual lapses with men were treated no more harshly than lapses with women. That policy did not last but it is important to realize that there were periods of toleration and that there have always been gay clergy. However, it is also important to realize that in describing men like Aelred as 'homosexual' we are interpreting his life in terms that would have been foreign to him. The very word 'homosexual' was coined in the nineteenth century and the idea that some people are oriented emotionally and sexually towards members of their own sex is quite a new discovery. Up until very recent times it was believed that all people were born oriented towards members of the opposite sex. Engaging in homosexual acts was therefore seen as being a deliberate perversion of one's own nature. The Penny Catechism, still used in Britain and Ireland in the early 1960s, described sodomy as one of the four sins crying to heaven for vengeance. The Church's assessment of how grave a sin this was varied over time. The Catholic Church in the eleventh and twelfth centuries did not see itself as having a gay clergy problem: it had a problem with clergy who were not chaste and slept with women or men. The question was whether those who broke their vows with women should be punished less harshly than those who had perverted nature and slept with men.

For the Catholic Church of our day the problem is much more

complicated than the breaking of vows and the severity of the sin. The modern human sciences, psychology and sociology, have taught us that there is such a thing as sexual orientation, that the majority of people are primarily oriented emotionally and sexually to members of the opposite sex and a minority of people are oriented emotionally and sexually towards members of the same sex. Some people are genuinely bisexual — attracted towards both sexes. Some people are asexual, that is, not sexually drawn to either sex, and there is some fluidity in sexual orientation. But homosexual people do exist — or to use the terms which have come to be preferred by those people themselves because they are less medical or genitally focused: gay and lesbian people do exist. (For details of the developing understanding of homosexuality in the human sciences see John J. McNeill, *The Church and the Homosexual* [3rd edition, Beacon Press, Boston, 1988], pp. 109–26.)

Recent studies of Catholic clergy in the United States of America have indicated that between 20 and 50 per cent are gay (Robert Nugent and Jeannine Gramick, *Building Bridges* [Twenty-Third Publications, Connecticut, 1992], p. 103). Even taking the lowest figure of 20 per cent the figures are remarkable for they far exceed the estimated percentage of gay men in the general population (which is around 5–10 per cent). This raises the obvious question 'Why are so many gay men attracted to the priesthood?' There are several possible answers to this question, none of them mutually exclusive. If the struggle to come to terms with being 'different' and 'unacceptable' and to integrate their sexuality into the rest of their being often leads lesbian and gay people to ask deep spiritual questions which can be avoided or postponed by heterosexual people and also forces them to throw themselves into the mercy and love of God, then it is hardly surprising that many gay men feel called to serve God in the Church. As Matthew Fox has noted:

> Like any member of an oppressed group, the homosexual will know a lot about darkness, loneliness, nothingness. And about letting go and letting be ... The sacrament of 'coming out' is a kind of letting go: a letting go of the images of personhood, sexuality, and self-hood that society has put on one in favour of trusting oneself enough to let oneself be oneself ... This emptying and letting go and letting be can lead either to a deeper and more vulnerable, more compassionate sense of belonging with others

who suffer unjustly — or it can lead to a cynicism, a rage, a hoarding of consumer idols including sexual consumerism on the part of the homosexual. (Matthew Fox, 'The Spiritual Journey of the Homosexual... and Just About Everyone Else' in Robert Nugent, *A Challenge to Love: Gay and Lesbian Catholics in the Church* [Crossroad, New York, 1989], p. 198)

The great psychoanalyst Carl Gustav Jung believed that homosexually oriented people were often endowed 'with a wealth of religious feelings, which help to bring the *ecclesia spiritualis* into reality, and a spiritual receptivity which makes them responsive to revelation' (C. G. Jung, *The Collected Works*, vol. 9 [Pantheon, New York, 1959], pp. 86–7). Anthropological studies have produced evidence which seems to confirm Jung's assessment of the particular qualities of lesbian and gay people. In some societies, such as the Native American tribes, lesbians and gay men are honoured as having a unique spiritual authority. Edward Wilson, an American biologist, claims to have discovered that there is a link between a homosexual orientation and an altruistic personality, which again might explain why gay men are attracted to Christian ministry (E. O. Wilson, *Sociobiology: The New Synthesis* [Cambridge, MA, 1975]).

More prosaically, for most of its history the Catholic Church has presented its members with two options for life, to live a consecrated life of celibacy or to marry, homosexual activity being condemned as sinful. Little wonder then that men not sexually attracted to women should choose the former option — some interpreting their lack of interest in women as in itself a call from God to enter the priesthood or religious life. This seems to have happened a great deal before it came to be generally accepted that not all people are heterosexual. When the Vatican authorities accepted the findings of modern science and acknowledged that some people are naturally homosexual — and this did not happen until the 1970s (see the Vatican's *Declaration on Certain Questions Concerning Sexual Ethics*, 1975) — it was decided that to be gay or lesbian was not a sin but that engaging in sexual activity with members of the same sex was. Since the Church called all homosexual people to be celibate, entering the priesthood or religious life became an honourable way of channelling one's sexuality for God's service. Some men undoubtedly still enter the priesthood or religious life in an attempt to escape from their sexuality, believing that the sacrament of ordination or the structure and security of religious life and the rule of celibacy will somehow dissolve their sexuality and protect them from temptation. And some gay men are attracted to the priesthood or religious life because of the all-male environment.

It is easy to analyse why gay Catholic men may find the priest-hood or religious life attractive but it would be foolish to think that their sense of vocation can be deconstructed to the point of non-existence. God does not override our personal needs, desires or hang-ups but works through them, sometimes using them. There have been too many gay priests who have lived good and creative lives, enriched the Church and brought salvation and liberation to others for the phenomenon to be brushed aside with psychological and sociological analysis. Today gay men in the Western world are not under the same pressure as their forebears to marry; even within the Catholic Church there are movements to recognize the God-givenness of lesbian and gay sexuality and the blessedness of homosexual relationships; so the priesthood or religious life is by no means the obvious choice of life for a gay Catholic man and yet still gay men are attracted to the priesthood and religious life. The most obvious conclusion to draw from all this is that God is calling many gay men to the priesthood or religious life. The Church authorities, however, will not 'own' this fact. Gay priests are considered an embarrassment and a problem, a problem which some in the Church would like to eradicate.

In a television interview the American Catholic theologian John McNeill was asked what would happen to a gay priest or brother who 'came out', that is, openly declared his sexuality. McNeill answered decisively 'He is on his way out'. McNeill speaks from personal experience: a member of the Society of Jesus for nearly forty years, he was expelled from the Jesuits in 1987 for being openly gay and championing the cause of lesbian and gay people in the Catholic Church, arguing for the goodness of their sexuality and relationships. Gay priests are a problem for the Vatican because gay and lesbian lay people are a problem: their existence is recognized but their relation-ships and sexual activity are not. The Church has a problem about what is acceptable sexual activity for anyone. Gay priests are also a problem because all priests take a vow of celibacy which rules out any sexual activity. Therefore, the naming of sexual orientation is felt to be at best irrelevant or bad form; at worst, a drawing of attention to a priest's sexuality which should be sublimated.

Vatican teaching on homosexuality

In October 1986 the Congregation for the Doctrine of Faith (formerly the Holy Office) issued a paper entitled *Letter to the Bishops of the Catholic Church on the Pastoral Care of Homosexual Persons*. The Congregation's task is to protect the Church's teaching on all matters from heresy and in doing so the Congregation shares with the Pope and bishops in the Church's teaching office, the 'magisterium'. On 1 October 1986 Pope John Paul II granted Cardinal Ratzinger, the Prefect of the Congregation, an audience and approved the letter and ordered its publication. There can be no doubt that the letter is a highly authoritative, 'magisterial', document but it is not an infallible document. It remains the work of the Congregation for the Doctrine of Faith. It is not irreformable or protected from error and as such does not preclude further study of the subject. However, since the publication of what became known as the 'Halloween letter' (because of the date on which it was released) a number of Catholic theologians who have attempted to test and refine the teaching contained in the letter have been censured, even silenced, by the Congregation for the Doctrine of Faith. These theologians include Charles Curran, Matthew Fox, John McNeill and André Guindon. Curran had acknowledged homosexual acts to be wrong but argued that in a sinful and imperfect world in which not all are able to realize the ideal of male–female relationships sexual activity in the context of a permanent and loving lesbian or gay relationship can be good. The Congregation has been acting as though the letter were infallible. This has only aggravated the fear and anger amongst gay and lesbian Catholics that was engendered by its contents.

The letter was essentially a rap on episcopal knuckles, a public call to Catholic bishops to come to order over the issue of homosexuality. Over ten years earlier in 1975 the Congregation issued a *Declaration on Certain Questions Concerning Sexual Ethics*. In preparing the declaration the Congregation attempted to come to grips with the huge advances in the understanding of sexuality which had been made in the twentieth century. For the first time in Catholic teaching a distinction was drawn between the homosexual condition or orientation and homosexual sexual behaviour. It seemed to imply that being lesbian or gay may not be sinful in itself but that giving in to homosexual desire and engaging in homosexual acts most certainly is. The declaration insisted, however, that 'homosexuals must certainly be treated with understanding' and suggested that Catholics should be cautious in judging even those who did engage in homosexual sex. The Congregation also encouraged further study of sexual issues in the Church:

> The traditional doctrine must be studied more deeply. It must be handed on in a way capable of properly informing the consciences of those confronted with new situations and enriched with a discernment of all elements that can usefully and truthfully be brought forward about the meaning and value of human sexuality.

During the ten years between the issuing of the 1975 declaration and the 1986 letter a great deal of further study on the issue of homosexuality took place within the Catholic Church. Lesbian and gay Catholics began to organize themselves into support groups and some entered into dialogue with local bishops. Some Catholic theologians began to suggest that homosexual acts might also be regarded as neutral in themselves.

In 1976 the Catholic bishops of the United States published a letter on moral values, *To Live in Christ Jesus*, which contained only one paragraph on homosexuality. However, this one paragraph called upon the Church to focus less on orientation and genital acts when discussing homosexuality. It suggested that the time had come to focus on pastoral care, human and civil rights and homophobia — a pathological fear of homosexuality which often manifests itself in aggressive verbal and physical mistreatment of gay and lesbian people.

In 1979 the Social Welfare Commission of the Catholic bishops of England and Wales published *An Introduction to the Pastoral Care of Homosexual People*. It was a well-informed, pastorally sensitive and carefully written work which acknowledged:

> As a group that has suffered more than its share of oppression and contempt, the homosexual community has a particular claim upon the concern of the Church. Homosexuals have a right to enlightened and effective pastoral care with pastoral ministers who are properly trained to meet their pastoral needs.

The bishops condemned all injustice against gay and lesbian people and saw one of the Church's roles to be to help people to 'come out' and integrate their sexuality within their whole being. The bishops asserted that 'Homosexuality (or homophilia) as such is neither morally good nor bad . . . It is morally neutral . . .' and they hinted at the possibility that in some circumstances homosexual behaviour within the context of a stable relationship may not be sinful: 'While the objective norms are clear-cut the application of such norms may be complicated.'

The AIDS crisis which began in the early 1980s brought out the best and the worst in the Catholic Church. Some bishops, priests and religious welcomed it as God's judgement on homosexuals. Others responded compassionately to human need and for the first time became involved with the gay community and were deeply impressed by the love they found there. They found that they could no longer dismiss this love as sinful.

The study of the issue by other Christian denominations also influenced many Catholic theologians, the Second Vatican Council having encouraged closer co-operation and greater respect between the Catholic Church and other Churches. The Anglican Communion in Britain and the United States was reviewing traditional teaching on homosexuality in the light of modern scientific evidence and human experience. And non-Catholic theologians were producing books on the topic which raised questions about the traditional interpretation of certain scriptural passages and standard theological arguments.

It was in reaction to the direction which discussion on homosexuality was taking that the 1986 Vatican letter was written. The fact that it was first written in English and not in Latin or Italian reveals that it was aimed directly at the English-speaking countries. Those bishops who had described the homosexual condition as morally neutral were rebuked in no uncertain terms:

> In the discussion which followed the publication of the Declaration, however, an overtly benign interpretation was given to the homosexual condition itself, some going so far as to call it neutral, or even good. Although the particular inclination of the homosexual person is not a sin, it is a more or less strong tendency ordered toward an intrinsic moral evil; and thus the inclination itself must be seen as an objective disorder.

The letter goes on to argue that Scripture and the Church's tradition testify to the fact that homosexual activity is sinful because it is incapable of transmitting new life. The Church's ministers are instructed to avoid becoming involved in supporting changes to civil statutes and laws to end discrimination against gay and lesbian people.

> This [the effort to involve the Church in the civil rights movement] is done to conform to these pressure groups' concept that homosexuality is at least a completely harmless, if not an entirely good, thing. Even when the practice of homosexuality may seriously threaten the lives and well-being of a large number of people [presumably a reference to AIDS], its advocates remain undeterred and refuse to consider the magnitude of the risks involved.

Although the Church has a duty to speak out against violence towards lesbian and gay people, the letter also states that in many respects gay and lesbian people have themselves to blame for violent expression of homophobia:

> When such a claim is made [that the homosexual condition is not disordered] and when homosexual activity is consequently condoned, or when civil legislation is introduced to protect behaviour to which no one has any conceivable right, neither the Church nor society at large should be surprised when other disordered notions and practices gain ground, and irrational and violent reactions increase.

The only life open to a gay or lesbian person wishing to be faithful to the Church is one of chastity. The bishops are told in the letter that they have the 'particularly grave responsibility' to see to it that priests are well schooled in Church teaching and 'personally disposed' to teach it. Bishops are forbidden to support any group which does not defend Church teaching.

> All support should be withdrawn from any organizations which seek to undermine the teaching of the Church, which are ambiguous about it, or which neglect it entirely. Such support, or even the semblance of such support, can be gravely misinterpreted. Special attention should be given to the practice of scheduling religious services and to the use of Church buildings by these groups, including the facilities of Catholic schools and colleges.

This instruction was a thinly disguised attack on bishops in the

United States, some of whom had allowed Dignity, an affirming support and campaigning group for lesbian and gay Catholics, to use Church premises to meet and worship in and allowed priests to become pastors of the various chapters of Dignity. After the publication of the 1986 letter Dignity found themselves evicted from many Church premises, dialogue with bishops was suspended and many priests who had been openly supportive of its aims were censured.

In the USA bishops sympathetic to the lesbian and gay cause gradually got around the 1986 letter by establishing public, diocesan-sponsored ministries to lesbian and gay Catholics which avoided challenging Church teaching. Whilst the bishops had to tread carefully, a growing number of national Catholic institutions began to support publicly human and civil rights for lesbian and gay people. In 1990, however, the bishops bravely issued a new document on human sexuality, *Human Sexuality: A Catholic Perspective for Education and Lifelong Learning*, which contained a section on homosexuality. Conservative and liberal bishops clashed over the wording of this section but the final version was a cautious piece which called for respect, justice and friendship for gay and lesbian people, condemned homophobia and, whilst repeating Vatican teaching on the subject, acknowledged that 'the process of moving from absolute values to general norms to specific case judgements requires the virtue of prudence' and that each man or woman must 'discern his or her own moral decisions'. The bishops also acknowledged that the distinction between orientation and acts as 'not always clear and convincing'.

There were some well-intentioned attempts to argue that the 1986 letter was not actually as bad as it sounded to lesbian and gay people. Archbishop Quinn of San Francisco wrote the following on the description of the homosexual inclination as 'an objective disorder':

> This is philosophical language. The inclination is a disorder because it is directed to an object that is disordered. The inclination and the object are in the same order philosophically. But 'the particular inclination of the homosexual person is not a sin'. In trying to understand this affirmation, we should advert to two things. First, every person has disordered inclinations. For instance, the inclination to rash judgement is disordered, the inclination to cowardice, the inclination to hypocrisy — these are all

disordered inclinations. Consequently, homosexual persons are not the only ones who have disordered inclinations. Second, the letter does not say that the homosexual person is disordered. The inclination, not the person, is described as disordered ... the document affirms the spiritual and human dignity of the homosexual *person* while placing a negative moral judgement on homosexual *acts* and a negative philosophical judgement on the homosexual *inclination* or orientation, which it clearly states is not a sin or moral evil. (John R. Quinn, 'Towards an Understanding of the Letter *On the Pastoral Care of Homosexual Persons*' in Jeannine Gramick and Pat Furey, *The Vatican and Homosexuality: Reactions to the 'Letter to the Bishops of the Catholic Church on the Pastoral Care of Homosexual Persons'* [Crossroad, New York, 1988], pp. 16–17)

However, whilst the more liberal bishops of the United States attempted to undo some of the distrust and fear of the Church that had gripped the gay and lesbian community after the 1986 letter, by supporting anti-discrimination legislation, the Congregation for the Doctrine of Faith was regrouping for another assault which demonstrated that it did not in fact make the subtle distinctions such as Archbishop Quinn had argued for.

In July 1992 the Congregation for the Doctrine of Faith issued another document on homosexuality, although this time the document was not presented to or signed by the Pope and was only addressed to Catholic bishops in the United States. In *Some Considerations Concerning the Catholic Response to Legislative Proposals on the Non-Discrimination of Homosexual Persons* the Vatican offered 'discreet' advice to the bishops on how they should react to proposed legislation which would make discrimination on the grounds of sexuality illegal. The document instructed bishops actively to oppose such legislation: remaining neutral was not good enough. The thrust of the document was that lesbian and gay people have no absolute human or civil rights because they are 'objectively disordered' and a danger to society.

'Sexual orientation' does not constitute a quality comparable to race, ethnic background etc. in respect to non-discrimination. Unlike these, homosexual orientation is an objective disorder and evokes moral concern.

There are areas in which it is not unjust discrimination to take sexual orientation into account, for example, in the placement of children for adoption or foster care, in employment of teachers or athletic coaches, and in military recruitment.

Homosexual persons, as human persons, have the same rights as all persons, including the right of not being treated in a manner which offends their personal dignity. Among other rights, all persons have the rights to work, to housing, etc. Nevertheless, these rights are not absolute. They can be legitimately limited for objectively disordered external conduct. This is sometimes not only licit but obligatory. This would obtain moreover not only in the case of culpable behaviour but even in the case of actions of the physically or mentally ill. Thus it is accepted that the state may restrict the exercise of the rights, for example, in the case of contagious or mentally ill persons, in order to protect the common good.

The authors of the document claim that it is only those lesbians and gay men 'who assert their homosexuality' or reveal it by their conduct who suffer discrimination as most homosexual people do not disclose their orientation and therefore 'the problem of discrimination in terms of employment, housing etc. does not usually arise'. Those who do suffer discrimination therefore bring it upon themselves. The only gay or lesbian people who have rights to housing and employment are those who hide their orientation. The bishops were to oppose any legislation which would 'protect homosexual acts' or partnerships. 'There is no right to homosexuality.'

Between 1975 and 1992 the Vatican hardened its line on homosexuality to the point that it has come to state that gay and lesbian people, whether chaste or not, are a danger to society in that they threaten the 'common good' by undermining the family upon which the Church believes society is built and so disordered that if they insist upon being open about their sexuality they have to be deprived of their human and civil rights. Between 1975 and 1986 the theoretical obstacles to gay men becoming priests or brothers were few. The 1975 letter had declared that homosexual acts were disordered but the condition itself not sinful, therefore in theory there could be no theological objections to gay men offering themselves for the priesthood or religious life as long as they pledged themselves to live chaste, celibate lives. Of course, homophobia was still rife within the Church and gay seminarians and priests were still not safe enough to 'come out' publicly, but the 1975 letter created an atmosphere of hope and freed moral theologians like Curran to address the issue of homosexuality in a compassionate fashion. But the 1986 letter changed everything. As William Hart McNichols SJ has put it:

> What has been poured into Catholicism again, and had been largely and mercifully absent for almost twenty years, is a palpable sense of fear. People fear the hierarchy again. They fear the vigilante terrorist groups who sell souls to authorities in the name of orthodoxy. They fear again even the word *church*. ('A Priest Forever' in Jeannine Gramick, *Homosexuality in the Priesthood and the Religious Life* [Crossroad, New York, 1989], p. 121)

This fear not only surrounds the issue of homosexuality. During the pontificate of Pope John Paul II the vision and ideas for institutional renewal brought to birth by the Second Vatican Council at times can seem to have been systematically ignored and stamped upon. Certainly the Council's endorsement of theological pluralism and its vision of a Church in which laity and priesthood inform, educate and empower each other has been crushed by the Congregation for the Doctrine of Faith's attempts to wipe out dissent and pluralism, in what has become a heresy hunt centred upon the liberation theologians of Latin America and moral theologians in the West. Women, liberation theologians and gay and lesbian people have been the main victims of the change in attitude and atmosphere that has swept through the Vatican.

In 1986 suddenly all homosexual people, whether living celibate lives or not, were suffering from 'an objective disorder'. Then the 1992 letter declared gay and lesbian people to be dangerous to society in general and the family in particular. Could people suffering from such a disorder be priests or religious representing Christ to the world? This question had raised its head in the 1980s when surveys among priests and religious in the United States first exposed the extraordinary number of gay men in Catholic ministry, and support groups and organizations for gay Catholic priests and religious began to be founded. A year before the 1986 letter was published Cardinal Silvio Oddi of the Vatican Congregation for the Clergy spoke to a gathering of thousands of priests from all over the world and said 'Candidates for the priesthood must be wisely culled, with particular attention paid to character weaknesses occasioned by the unnatural tendencies common in contemporary society' (Robert Nugent, 'Homosexuality and Seminary Candidates' in Jeannine Gramick, *Homosexuality in the Priesthood and the Religious Life* [Crossroad, New York, 1989], pp. 205–6). In 1985 Cardinal Baum, Prefect of the Congregation for Catholic Education, published *A Memorandum to Bishops Seeking Advice in Matters Concerning Homosexuality and Candidates for Admission to Seminary*, in which he anticipated the conclusions of the 1986 Ratzinger letter by refusing to acknowledge that the homosexual orientation in itself might be neutral. Those applicants who were sexually active homosexuals or those who exhibited a homosexual orientation were not to be admitted to seminary. Baum's position was expanded upon in a statement issued from the US Bishops' Committee of Priestly Formation which made a distinction between those homosexual candidates who are 'ego-dystonic' — men who find their sexuality a grave problem which causes them distress, sorrow and guilt and who seek to change their orientation — and those who are 'ego-syntonic' — those who have accepted their orientation and do not wish to see it changed. The committee suggested that only those homosexual men who were ego-dystonic should be admitted to seminary. In 1990 the Congregation for Institutes of Consecrated Life and Societies of Apostolic Life issued *Directives on Formation in Religious Institutes* which included the following statement in a section on sexuality and formation:

> reasons must be given and understood to explain why those who do not seem to be able to overcome their homosexual tendencies, or who maintain that it is possible to adopt a third way 'living in an ambiguous state between celibacy and marriage' must be dismissed from the religious life.

Again the assumption is that even those homosexual men and women who manage to live celibate lives are as much a threat to religious life as those, heterosexual or homosexual, who do not. It is clear then that the Vatican wants homosexual men, whether celibate or not, weeded out from the priesthood and religious life, and that this is a desire shared by some Catholic bishops. Considering the Vatican's stance on homosexuality since 1986 this position is perfectly consistent and logical. But there are many in the Catholic Church who do not find the 1986 letter theologically convincing nor its stance on gay priests acceptable.

A different approach

There are an increasing number of Roman Catholic bishops, priests, theologians and members of the laity who find themselves dissenting from the Vatican's statements on homosexuality. In one of the most comprehensive and detailed analyses of the Church's teaching on sexuality Gareth Moore, a British Dominican, has subjected the teaching contained in the 1986 letter to the logic of reason. He claims that the magisterium presents arguments which are based upon distorted readings of Scripture, an intellectually dubious assessment of what is 'natural' and arguments which are so unconvincing that they merely discredit the Church's position in the eyes of the world. The scriptural injunctions against homosexuality in the Holiness Code of the Old Testament and Paul's letters cannot simply be used, Moore argues, without recognizing that they were developed within a social context very different to our own. Ancient Israelite society was patriarchal, that is, based upon the assumption that man is superior to woman. Power lay in the hands of the male. For a man to take on the passive role in sexual intercourse was to take on the woman's role and thereby demean himself and all men and to subvert the social order which was based on a rigid distinction between men and women. For ancient Israelite society male homosexuality (there is no mention of female homosexuality) was so repulsive because it involved the humiliating of one who was supposed to be dominant. But the Christian Gospel subverts the assumptions upon which the condemnation of male homosexuality in Leviticus 18:22 is based. For the Christian proclaims:

> There is no longer Jew or Greek, there is no longer slave or free, there is no longer male and female; for all of you are one in Christ Jesus. (Galatians 3:28)

Moore explains:

> Beyond relations between the sexes, it is clear that for Christians society cannot be based on the dominance of any group over another; Christian society is rather to be based on service ... Because we want a different kind of society from that in and for which the law of Leviticus 18:22 was framed, we cannot uncritically take over that law or any other from the same source into our sexual ethic ... In a Christian society, if a man lies with a man

as with a woman, and so treats him as a woman, he does not thereby demean him; neither does the other demean himself. (Gareth Moore, *The Body in Context: Sex and Catholicism* [SCM, London, 1992], pp. 41–2)

Similarly, Dr William Countryman in a study of sexual ethics in the New Testament and their application today pointed out that a careful study of Paul's condemnation of homosexuality in Romans 1 reveals that Paul did not regard homosexuality as a sin in itself but as a punishment visited upon Gentiles for their sin of idolatry. Paul clearly refers to homosexual acts as impure rather than sinful. But one of the main themes of Paul's theology is that part of the revelation brought by Christ is that nothing in itself is unclean. That is not to say that nothing in itself is sinful — anything which contradicts the law of love is sinful — but just that the clean/unclean categories can no longer be used by a follower of Christ. So, Countryman concludes, Paul's condemnation of homosexuality as unclean cannot be used with integrity to label as sinful the relationships of gay men and lesbian women. Daniel Maguire summarizes the point being made by Moore and Countryman about the Church's scriptural inheritance:

What modern Catholicism inherited was a hodgepodge heavily marked by taboo thinking. Taboo is not concerned with the two marks of sin: *real unnecessary harm* and *unreasonableness*. It doesn't look to harm or reason as criteria. Taboo says that something is wrong because it is forbidden by the powers that be, regardless of whether it is harmful or unreasonable ... A sexual ethic is best founded on justice, not taboo. *Justice is the virtue whereby we render to each his or her own with an eye to the common good.* (Daniel C. Maguire, 'The Shadow Side of the Homosexuality Debate' in Jeannine Gramick, *Homosexuality in the Priesthood and the Religious Life*, p. 46)

Moore also attacks the theory of complementarity which lies at the heart of the 1986 letter. The thesis upon which this theory is based is that God creates humankind in his own image as male and female. Male and female are therefore complementary and reflect the image of their creator when they come together in the transmission of life. Since homosexual activity does not bring together male and female or lead to reproduction, it is a disordered use of human sexuality.

Moore believes this argument to be severely flawed on several counts. First, the theory of complementarity only works if we ignore the fact that not all humanity is created male or female, some people are hermaphrodites. Secondly, the most obvious reading of Genesis 1:27 upon which the Vatican theologians build their theory of complementarity is not the one they give but the affirmation of the equality of women with men: both are made in the image of God. Thirdly, the Vatican's theory seems to imply that men and women are incomplete without each other:

> But a man is in no clear sense part of a woman, nor a woman part of a man. Unlike a man who lacks an arm, a man who lacks a woman does not lack part of himself; he lacks somebody else. When people lack other people it is not their wholeness that is in question so much as their needs. (p. 118)

Moore also points out that the idea that it is in male–female complementarity that we image God is a very novel theory. Both Augustine and Aquinas believed that the image of God lies in our ability to reason.

He also exposes the weaknesses of the Vatican's insistence that sex must always be open to the possibility of conception, any other form of sexual activity being sinful. He claims that the origins of this belief lie in the early Church's assimilation of Greek, particularly Stoic, philosophy which was based upon a dualistic attitude to the body. Human beings were considered to be made up of two entities, body and soul. The fallen body was regarded as corrupt, uncontrollable and constantly dragging the soul downwards away from God. Salvation came through controlling and conquering the body in order that the soul might eventually be released and return to God. Sex like food and drink should only be taken to ensure life, anything more is dangerous self-indulgence which puts the soul in peril. Moore demolishes this argument by simply asking why, if sex for pleasure alone is illegitimate, should it be a pleasure at all? We do not need pleasure to do necessary things, we just need to be convinced that they are necessary.

> Doing things because we delight in them — i.e. for no particular reason at all — is central to human living. And it is essential to it; if we do not do it, we languish ... From the fact that food and drink are necessary to the survival of the individual it does not follow,

then, that our eating and drinking should be limited to what will enable us as individuals to survive. Similarly, though sex is necessary for the survival of the species, that is no reason to say that sexual activity should be limited to what is necessary for the species to survive. To have sex beyond necessity is to appreciate it as a good in itself, one of the things that contribute to the festal quality of human life and make it a desirable thing that the species survive. (pp. 68–9)

Moore believes that the words of God in Genesis 1:28, 'Be fruitful and multiply', are not a command but a blessing, because children were regarded as such in Israelite society. They are not words which define God's purpose for human sexuality but words which express God's delight in his creation. Of course the Catholic Church has long maintained that sex should be confined to marriage and therefore, if for no other reason, homosexual sex is illegitimate. Pope John Paul II and other Catholic theologians have argued that sexual activity must be confined to marriage because sex is a language of total commitment and can only be honestly 'said' within the married relationship. Moore attacks this argument for being based on the assumption that sex has a meaning independent of the parties involved and the context in which it takes place, when this simply does not reflect reality and experience. Sex can mean many things and this is entirely dependent upon the context within which the sexual gestures are made. While sexual conformity can express social conformity, sexual nonconformity is a natural way of express-ing social disaffection. Sex, Moore argues, is usually a gesture of personal closeness, a gesture of friendship. Marriage can certainly be one form of friendship but there are plenty of other forms. The joy of sex is a joy of two people involved in one shared activity which brings them pleasure and expresses their love for one another: 'A sexual encounter that neglects the importance of friendship is therefore defective, as is the pleasure that is derived from it' (p. 55). Casual sexual encounters and masturbation therefore have limited value and sexual relationships which are based upon use, abuse and violence are totally unacceptable for that is to misuse the gift God has given us, the gift to express our love for one another through our bodies and in doing so experience something of God's love and friendship.

Notions of nature and what is 'natural' or 'unnatural' behaviour have been used for centuries to condemn homosexuality. Moore regards these notions as an extremely weak basis upon which to condemn lesbian and gay people and their relationships as these notions are socially controlled and constructed.

> We do not just observe; we classify some things as natural and others as unnatural, for various purposes. What we find natural and unnatural depends very largely on what our society teaches us to find natural or unnatural, and that will reflect other values of dominant social groups. (p. 72)

So in a patriarchal society men who love men and women who love women will be regarded as 'unnatural' because they undermine the ideology upon which society is built.

Ironically, Moore agrees with Ratzinger that the distinction between orientation and practice is false. Such a distinction is based on a false dualism which has no grounding in the Old Testament or in Jesus' teaching.

> What and how we are, whether we are loving and saintly or mean and evil, is a matter of how we normally, habitually act. To be a particular kind of person is to be one who habitually acts in a particular way or range of ways. (p. 4)

Moore systematically exposes the irrationality and weakness of the Vatican's case against homosexuality. He argues that the Church's sexual ethic should be based upon living the life of the kingdom of God. This is the Christian vocation to live as if the kingdom inaugurated by Christ has come, for in doing so we hasten its arrival. The kingdom is about living in relationships. It is about treating people as they deserve, as beings made in the image of God. That means treating them with love and justice. Only by experiencing and giving love do we grow into the being we were created to be. This is what the scriptures mean by 'fruitfulness'. Whereas for centuries the Church has interpreted this in terms of fecundity, a fruitful life in scriptural terms is in fact a life of love, creativity and justice.

> Since human fruitfulness is so various, the possibility arises that human sexual activity can contribute to that fruitfulness in various ways, and not just through procreation... If what a person does sexually makes him more loving, generous and

considerate, then his sex life is genuinely fruitful in a Christian sense, even though it may never result in children, and even though it be of a type that could never do so. (p. 138)

It is on this basis alone, Moore argues, that sexual activity should be judged by the Church — does it bear fruit, does it make a person and his or her sexual partner happy, loving, creative, just and so on? Does it make them 'kingdom people' or not? On this basis the Church cannot justify writing all lesbians and gay men off as 'objectively disordered' or their sexual loving as 'an intrinsic moral evil'. For many lesbian and gay relationships 'bear fruit'. Moore concludes with endearing understatement, 'The Church needs to do more thinking about sex' (p. 213).

In the persons of theologians like Moore the Church is doing more thinking about sex. It is the Vatican which is refusing to think or to listen to these theologians. Some bishops, however, are resisting the Vatican's encouragement of witch-hunting.

In Britain the Catholic bishops did not react publicly to the 1986 letter and are rumoured to have resisted pressure from Rome to revise their 1979 pastoral guidelines to bring them into line with the Congregation for the Doctrine of Faith's views. Quest and the Roman Catholic Caucus of the Lesbian and Gay Christian Movement, two groups for lesbian and gay Catholics, function without episcopal censure and indeed Quest, which is the more conservative of the two groups, enjoys some measure of semi-official approval from the bishops. But there is still fear and uncertainty around, fear at how long the bishops can resist pressure from Rome and fear of who might replace the bishops when they retire. And there is still a great deal of anger at the tone and content of the 1986 letter. In Britain national Catholic organizations have not yet taken up the cause of lesbian and gay rights, with the result that, although many bishops are 'known' to be sympathetic, there is a distinct lack of overt official support. There is no feeling that the plight of gay and lesbian people is really known and appreciated in the Catholic Church in Britain. Some gay and lesbian Catholics would agree that silence is better than condemnation; others argue that silence in the face of homophobia is inexcusable since it encourages the perpetrators and increases the isolation of the victims and potential victims.

As far as the situation of gay priests and religious is concerned there are undoubtedly in Britain bishops, religious superiors and seminary rectors who would align themselves with Moore or Curran rather than the Vatican over the issue of homosexuality, believing that to be gay is not to be disordered but simply part of a minority which in itself is not a barrier to entering the priesthood or religious life. Here the teaching of the Second Vatican Council on priesthood is influential. In the conciliar decree on the ministry and life of priests, *Presbyterorum Ordinis*, the language used indicated a shift in emphasis in the understanding of the nature of priesthood. No longer was the term *sacerdos* used for priest. This is a cultic term and reflects an understanding of the priesthood which dominated the Catholic Church for centuries. This is drawn largely from the Hebrew scriptures where the priest is the man chosen to act as mediator between God and humankind primarily through the cult. The priest was a man 'set apart' from the rest of God's people and in the ancient Israelite society, which was dominated by notions of purity, the priest was to be the purest of the pure. This involved keeping himself apart from the rest of society and embodying purity in his person and actions.

> Speak to the priests, the sons of Aaron, and say to them: ... No one ... who has a blemish may approach to offer the food of his God. For no one who has a blemish shall draw near, one who is blind or lame, or one who has a mutilated face or a limb too long, or one who has a broken foot or a broken hand, or a hunchback, or a dwarf, or a man with a blemish in his eyes or an itching disease or scabs or crushed testicles. (Leviticus 21:1, 17–20)

This model of the priest as personally pure and separate from others, acting as a mediator between God and his people in the liturgy, was taken over by the Church. Whilst the Catholic Church was working with this model of priesthood all those suffering from physical or emotional 'disorders' were barred from ordination. However, during the 1950s some Catholic theologians began to advance an alternative model of priesthood. They pointed out that, whilst the New Testament may use sacerdotal language of Jesus and of the Church as a whole, it never uses such language with reference to the Church's ministers. The Christian priesthood, they pointed out, developed out of the office of presbyter, which in turn developed out of the synagogue. The presbyter was an elder who undertook administrative and pastoral responsibilities within the Church. In the

Latin text of *Presbyterorum Ordinis, presbyter* is used as the term for priest, not *sacerdos*. The emphasis was therefore taken off the personal purity of the priest and put on to his pastoral role. It is in his solidarity and unity with his people that the priest exercises his ministry, not in his separateness.

This new emphasis should have made it easier for gay men to become priests and religious. But the atmosphere created throughout the Church by the 1986 letter, which some have compared to the fear felt by those living under the rule of the Kremlin, means that few of those in positions of authority over priests and religious would dare to make known a positive theological and moral position on homosexuality and few seminarians or clergy would dare to admit their homosexuality for fear of being ejected or disciplined. The result is that gay seminarians and clergy suffer in silence, dreading discovery and exposure of their sexuality and are forced to lie to themselves or live a public lie. They carry this heavy burden on top of what is for many priests, including heterosexuals, a crushing burden, the discipline of celibacy.

The great illusion: clerical celibacy

Clerical celibacy has a long history that grew out of the disgust and fear of the body in general and sexuality in particular that gripped Christianity early in its history. It became mandatory for priests (and not just monks) at the Second Lateran Council in 1139, although there was a great deal of resistance to the rule for centuries. But Rome continued to insist upon clerical celibacy, at the very least, in order to avoid the perils of clerics passing down offices and Church property to their children and sexual scandal. Finally, at the Council of Trent in 1545, the last loophole was closed so that even men who had married before ordination were excluded from the priesthood. Celibacy and the priesthood were finally and definitively fused together (see Uta Ranke-Heinemann, *Eunuchs for Heaven: The Catholic Church and Sexuality* [André Deutsch, London, 1990], pp. 84–102).

Although canon law has always acknowledged celibacy to be a charism, a special gift from God, the Church came to believe that all those who were called to priesthood were also automatically recipients of this gift.

> Clerics are obliged to observe perfect and perpetual continence for the sake of the Kingdom of heaven, and are therefore bound to

celibacy. Celibacy is a special gift of God by which sacred ministers can more easily remain close to Christ with an undivided heart, and can dedicate themselves more freely to the service of God and their neighbour. (Canon 277)

So Catholic priests and religious came to be regarded as 'the third sex', sexless beings 'above' sexual desires and emotions. There have always been priests who could not remain celibate and there have always been scandals, but there has never been anything like the crisis which the Church faces today. Some men are undoubtedly called to celibacy and live good and fruitful lives enriched by this grace, but since the 1960s over 100,000 priests have left their ministry, many of them to marry. Studies carried out by the National Opinion Research Centre of Chicago in the 1970s revealed that most priests left their ministry not because of a desire to marry as such but because of the loneliness involved in being a priest and the lack of support from their superiors. Another report undertaken on behalf of American Catholic bishops in the late 1980s confirmed the findings of the earlier report but noted that it was not only personal struggles with sexuality that prompted some priests to leave but also 'issues surrounding feminism, married clergy, optional celibacy, and the role of homosexuals in ministry, to name but a few' (cited in Michael Gaine, 'The State of the Priesthood' in Adrian Hastings, *Modern Catholicism: Vatican II and After* [SPCK, London, 1991], p. 249). In 1990 an American lecturer in psychiatry, Richard Sipe, published the results of an in-depth survey of priests in the United States which revealed that 20 per cent of them were living in stable, sexually active relationships with women and a further 8–10 per cent were engaged in casual heterosexual contacts. Half of the homosexual clergy he studied were not celibate (Richard Sipe, *A Secret World: Sexuality and the Search for Celibacy* [Brunner/Mazel, New York, 1990]). Some priests argue that celibacy is not a commitment to abstain from all sexual relationships but simply a commitment to refrain from marriage and its responsibilities. The current crisis in celibacy has its origins in the sexual revolution of the 1960s and the reform of the Church through the Second Vatican Council. Vatican II broke down many of the barriers between clergy and laity and encouraged a collaborative ministry between the two. Priests and religious were encouraged to have much more contact with 'the world', a world which was becoming increasingly preoccupied with sex and which was questioning much about the Church, including its teaching on sexuality and celibacy. The women's movement attacked the Church's image of women as dangerous harlots out to tempt and defile men. At the same time, the Church began to promote marriage as the ideal relationship and in the glowing terms that had previously been only used of celibacy. Thousands of priests found their celibacy challenged personally and intellectually and discovered that they did not possess the charism which they had been taught came with the vocation to the priesthood. As thousands of priests and religious left their ministry, the number of vocations also diminished. In the Western world, at least, there are now far fewer priests to go around, with the result that it is now rare to find more than one priest living in a presbytery. Loneliness and isolation add to the strains on a priest's commitment to celibacy. But still the Church expects its priests to be celibate. They continue to be perceived as sexless, without emotional or physical needs, and it is always a shock when a scandal breaks. There are voices in the Church which call for the end of compulsory clerical celibacy, on the grounds that it has no basis in Scripture and that the Church managed for half its history without it. It is argued that enforcing celibacy on men who have a vocation to priesthood but not to celibacy is placing too heavy a burden on their shoulders which must damage their psychological well-being and impede their ministry. Obviously the situation is different for members of religious communities where the character and purpose of the community requires the single-minded commitment of its members.

The Vatican, however, shows no signs of reconsidering the relationship of celibacy and priesthood, although in 1968 the permanent diaconate was reintroduced and opened to married men, and since 1952 special permission has been given on occasion for married Lutheran and Anglican ministers who have converted to Catholicism to be reordained (an action which has caused some resentment amongst former and current Catholic priests). Since the Vatican's position on priestly celibacy is unlikely to change in the immediate future, people involved in the training and formation of priests and religious have come to see the importance of preparing candidates for celibacy. Richard Sipe has written:

> The Church requires celibacy of its priests but neither trains them for it nor supports them effectively. Serious, explicit, and in-depth

attention to education for celibacy is necessary. ('Sex and Celibacy', *The Tablet*, 9 May 1992, p. 576)

This will involve proper sexual education, a historical knowledge of celibacy, learning from the experiences of others and an enormous amount of self-exploration which will include exploration of sexual orientation and sexual drive. This is a need acknowledged by Pope John Paul in an encyclical entitled *Pastores Dabo Vobis: Apostolic Exhortation of His Holiness John Paul II on the Formation of Priests*, 1992.

> Education for responsible love and the affective maturity of the person are totally necessary for those who, like the priest, are called to *celibacy* ... Since the charism of celibacy, even when it is genuine and has proved itself, leaves man's affections and his instinctive impulses intact, candidates to the priesthood need an affective maturity which is prudent, able to renounce anything that is a threat to it, vigilant over both body and spirit, and capable of esteem and respect in interpersonal relationships between men and women ... The seminarian should have a sufficient degree of psychological and sexual maturity as well as an assiduous and authentic life of prayer ... For a deeper understanding of man and the phenomena and lines of development of society, in relation to a pastoral ministry which is as 'incarnate' as possible, the so-called '*human sciences*' can be of considerable use, sciences such as sociology, psychology, education, economics and politics, and the science of social communication. (pp. 120–43)

But it is not only clergy who have to be educated if celibacy is going to work. The usual justification for priestly celibacy is that it enables the priest to devote himself entirely to the service of the Church, his people. To be a celibate is not to be a bachelor, it is to be in relationship with the people one is called to serve.

> A priest is meant to be one who is passionately in love with his people. His whole life is to be centred around his relationship with his people ... Celibacy is a charism of relationship, not a sentence to loneliness ... When living in relationship with his people, his basic human emotional needs for love, belonging, self-worth and autonomy will be met. (Charles A. Gallagher and

Thomas L. Vandenberg, *The Celibacy Myth: Loving for Life* [Crossroad, New York, 1988], pp. 36–43)

For celibacy to work, then, the priest must be in relationship with his people, they must let him into their lives and recognize his needs. John Paul II underlined this in his exhortation on priestly formation.

> ... the very exercise of the pastoral ministry leads to a constant and fruitful mutual exchange between the priest's life of faith and that of the laity. Indeed *the very relationship and sharing of life between the priest and the community*, if it is wisely conducted and made use of, will be a *fundamental contribution* to permanent formation, which cannot be reduced to isolated episodes or initiatives, but covers the whole ministry and life of the priest ... Even the doubts, crises and hesitations in the face of all kinds of personal or social situations, the temptation to rejection or despair at times of pain, illness, death: all the difficult circumstances which people find in their path as Christians are fraternally lived and sincerely suffered in the priest's heart... And so the entire People of God, in each and every one of its members, can and should offer precious assistance to the ongoing formation of its priests ... They should establish cordial and brotherly relations with them, helping priests to remember that they are not to 'lord it over' the faithful, but rather 'work with them for their joy'. (pp. 212–13)

This will require a great deal of re-education among the Catholic laity who usually only encounter their priest for less than an hour on a Sunday morning, see their priests come and go, have never been encouraged to get close to their pastor and suspect those that do of seeking to compromise his celibacy.

The gay priest, the Church and celibacy

One of the ways in which some leading Catholics in the United States have tried to deflect attention away from the celibacy crisis amongst clergy in general has been to try and focus attention on the number of homosexual priests, religious and seminarians, as if to imply that they alone are responsible for the crisis. Reports of seminary life being taken over by 'camp queens' reached the press. Stringent psychological tests, and even in some quarters HIV testing, have become part of the vetting procedures for candidates for the priesthood and religious life which many suspect were devised to weed out gay applicants or only take those who are ego-dystonic. However, all this is simply a recipe for disaster. Such tactics do not weed out gay men but they encourage them to hide their sexual orientation. A person who out of fear of rejection or expulsion does not disclose his sexual orientation cannot benefit from priestly formation. In *Pastores Dabo Vobis* John Paul II emphasizes the importance of emotional and sexual formation for seminarians and priests because it is their whole person that they bring to the priesthood and it is through their whole person that they minister to others.

[The] priest is chosen by Christ not as an 'object' but as a 'person'. In other words, he is not inert and passive, but rather is a 'living instrument'... In this way the exercise of his ministry deeply involves the priest himself as a conscious, free and responsible person. (p. 64)

... the human formation of the priest shows its special importance when related to the receivers of the mission: in order that his ministry may be humanly as credible and acceptable as possible, it is important that the priest should mould his human personality in such a way that it becomes a bridge and not an obstacle for others in their meeting with Jesus Christ the Redeemer of man. It is necessary that, following the example of Jesus who 'knew what was in man' (Jn 2:25, cf. 8:3–11), the priest should be able to know the depths of the human heart, to perceive difficulties and problems, to make meeting and dialogue easy, to create trust and cooperation, to express serene and objective judgements. Future priests should therefore cultivate a series of human qualities, not only out of proper and due growth and realization of self, but also with a view to ministry. These qualities are needed for them to be balanced people, strong and free, capable of bearing the weight of pastoral responsibilities. They need to be educated to love the truth, to be loyal, to respect every person, to have a sense of justice, to be true to their word, to be genuinely compassionate, to be men of integrity and, especially, to be balanced in judgement and behaviour... Of special importance is the capacity to relate to others... In this context affective maturity, which is the result of an education in true and responsible love, is a significant and decisive factor in the formation of candidates to the priesthood.

Affective maturity presupposes an awareness that love has a central role in human life... We are speaking of a love that involves the entire person, in all his aspects, physical, psychic and spiritual, and which is expressed in the 'nuptial meaning' of the human body, thanks to which a person gives himself to another and takes the other to himself. A properly understood sexual education leads to understanding and realizing this 'truth' about human love. (pp. 116–19)

The Pope's clear endorsement of a formation which concentrates on the candidate's sexuality and relationships reflects the extent to which he has been listening to those who, like Sipe, have argued that the present crisis in the priesthood is due in part, at least, to the fact that priests were not educated for celibacy and that in the sex-fearing atmosphere of the Church and seminary the development of their sexuality was denied and arrested at a very young age. The celibacy crisis has not been confined to the thousands of priests who leave their ministry to marry or to public discovery of gay priests. The past decade has seen the exposure of a frighteningly large number of cases of priests abusing children — a phenomenon which one is tempted to blame on the Church for failing to give priests the opportunity to explore their sexuality and grow in sexual maturity. The Pope's commitment to providing seminarians with appropriate emotional and sexual formation bodes well for the future for heterosexual priests but not for their gay brothers.

Since priestly ministry is essentially about relationships with God, with Christ, with the Church, with fellow priests and superiors and with the world, and a person's sexuality is the seat of relationality, the facility we use to relate to others not just sexually but emotionally and rationally, it is vital that a priest or religious should have come to terms with and explored his own sexuality, know something about sexuality in general and know how to relate to others using his sexuality. This is particularly important if a man is expected to learn how to be celibate for he will need to learn about his own sexual boundaries and those of others. But a seminarian who is afraid to disclose his sexuality or has only been accepted because he hates his sexuality will not be able to participate properly in or benefit from such formation, with the result that his ability to relate, love and bring his whole person to his priesthood or religious life will be impaired, perhaps dangerously so for himself and the people to whom he is called to minister. If a priest or religious is frightened of his sexuality then that will become an 'obstacle' in all his relationships. If homosexual priests and religious have more trouble with celibacy than their heterosexual brothers, as suggested in a recent survey by James Wolf (*Gay Priests* [Harper and Row, San Francisco, 1989], pp. 36–41), the cause may not lie in the common belief that gay men are naturally promiscuous and lack sexual control but in the sexual tensions that must arise when gay men find themselves living and working in an institution which is dominated by men and they have received no special training in celibacy.

Gay clergy: facing the truth

The Vatican will have to come to accept that there always have been and there always will be gay priests and religious. Witch-hunts only encourage secrecy and gay and lesbian people are experts in hiding their sexuality and pretending to be straight. This is what their experience of growing up in a homophobic secular world teaches them. There is also the often overlooked fact that the pace of sexual development is not uniform. Some men will not discover their sexuality until they enter seminary or even after ordination. And of course there are plenty of gay men who entered the Church's ministry long before homosexuality among clergy became an issue. The Church has chosen men who happen to be gay to be its priests and religious. It must face this truth for the sake of the 20 per cent (or more) of its clergy who are gay and need appropriate formation and support and for the sake of the faithful who deserve well-integrated and open pastors. It is ironic that Pope John Paul II should call upon the Church to learn from and make use of the human sciences in order to develop the best possible formation for priests and religious but choose to ignore the lessons that the human sciences have to teach about homosexuality. The human sciences have taught us that homosexuality is not a perversion but a natural condition for a minority of men and women. It was the human sciences that debunked the myth that homosexuals are mentally ill and can be 'cured'. Their work on homosexuality prompted the World Health Organization and the associations of British and

American psychiatrists to remove homosexuality from their lists of mental disorders. It is the human sciences that have explained the fear of homosexuality that accompanies a patriarchal society and which translates itself into homophobia, which in turn is rationalized into moral and 'scientific' reasons why homosexuality is 'perverted' and 'dangerous'. It is the human sciences that have taught us that gay men are not necessarily a danger to children. A greater percentage of heterosexuals abuse children than homosexuals. If the Pope is sincere in his desire for the Church to gain 'a deeper understanding of man and lines of development of society in relation to a pastoral ministry', through the use of sociology, psychology, education and so on, then one of the most important and urgent issues on which the human sciences should be consulted is homosexuality.

Sipe suggests that there are a small proportion of priests who do not have enough sexual experience to resolve for themselves their sexual identity and within a homosocial situation experience homosexual feelings. It would be wrong to label such men as homosexual because subsequent history and development can reveal an essentially heterosexual orientation and choice (*A Secret World*, pp. 123, 136). The Church authorities now accept that candidates for the priesthood must have achieved sexual maturity and know their sexual orientation and so the problem is not as great as it was in the past. But it points to the importance of giving men who have been ordained the opportunity to explore their sexuality.

God seems to be calling gay men to the priesthood and religious life. The Vatican and wider Church has to face this fact. This book has been written to encourage and help that process. Someone once wrote 'Argument provides argument, reason is met by sophistry. But narratives . . . go right to the heart.' In the end what will change the Vatican's attitude to homosexuality and gay clergy is not theological or philosophical argument but the experience of encountering gay and lesbian Catholics who live the life of the Gospel and gay clergy whose Christ-like lives and ministry meet humankind's need to

> come out of their anonymity and fear . . . to be known and called by name, to walk in safety along the paths of life, to be found again if they have become lost, to be loved, to receive salvation as the supreme gift of God's love. (*Pastores Dabo Vobis*, p. 221)

Unfortunately, because of the attitude to homosexuality prevalent in society as a whole and in the Church, fear stifles the voices of most gay and lesbian people. And it is only through projects of the kind upon which this book is based that those in places of power and influence can meet the experience of lesbians and gay people.

Chosen: the project

This book has been written so that the experience of gay Catholic clergy can be more widely known and understood by the Catholic Church. It is written primarily so that gay Catholic priests and seminarians should know that they are not alone. It also intends to inform those in authoritative positions in the Church of the concerns and needs of gay clergy and to educate the laity that they might take pastoral responsibility for their gay priests and religious. It is not in any sense a scientific survey. A questionnaire was devised by myself in consultation with Catholic clergy and sent out to priests, religious and seminarians through Quest and the Lesbian and Gay Christian Movement (LGCM). The questionnaire was simply offered as a starting-point and respondents were encouraged to expand upon it or ignore it altogether in order to tell their stories. 21 men responded. This figure might seem low but in a similar but much larger and more scientific project conducted in the United States James Wolf received 101 responses to his questionnaire. When one considers that the Catholic population of the United States is approximately ten times that of Britain then the response to our questionnaire is good. The fact that more replies were not received has more to do with fear of disclosure than the number of gay priests or seminarians. Respondents were self-selecting but replies were received from all over England and Scotland and from a wide age range. Four priests were trained and ordained in the 1950s and early 1960s before the Second Vatican Council, two had recently been ordained and the rest had been trained and ordained between the late 1960s and early 1980s. Three are members of religious orders. Replies were received from three seminarians, one of them training abroad. The overwhelming majority of the priest respondents are in parish work. Three are in chaplaincy work and one is a missionary. One had spent some years working in a seminary. Initially, I had intended simply to reproduce all the replies but since the replies vary in length, from one-line answers to the questionnaire and nothing more, to lengthy contributions, I have decided to reproduce in full four of the more lengthy replies which represent very different attitudes to sexuality and the priesthood. I have included all three of the seminarian replies in full, because these give some idea of the present attitudes to gay priests in the Church. I then quote from and analyse all the replies in terms of subject-matter. After this I draw some conclusions about the experiences, concerns and needs of gay priests in Britain and offer some recommendations to bishops, superiors and seminary rectors as to how they might offer pastoral support and proper formation for homosexual men chosen by God to be priests or religious.

Father Brian

Are you happy to be gay?
First of all, I object to the term 'gay' for all sorts of reasons — I think on the whole I am happy to be homosexual although this hasn't always been the case. A priest once said to me in the sacrament of reconciliation that whatever I was, hetero or homo, God made me, and whatever God made is good, therefore I am good and that my homosexuality has a purpose of some sort. I have had help coming to terms with my sexuality and my acceptance of it.

What is your view of the Church's teaching on homosexuality?
The Church's teaching has progressed from eternal damnation to at least acceptance of the homosexual state, if not the homosexual act. With the onslaught of AIDS the use of condoms is now accepted as the lesser of two evils — I'm not sure I consider homosexuality as evil. Individual pastors are more tolerant than others, perhaps realistic rather than tolerant. As with all matters sexual the Church presents an ideal point of view one can only hope to aspire to, whatever the inclination.

How did you react to the 1986 Letter on the Pastoral Care of Homosexual Persons?
As regards the 1986 letter on homosexuality, it came as no surprise that homosexual activity would not be acceptable — but at least homosexuals were acknowledged as needing pastoral care.

Did it change your behaviour and attitudes in any way?
No, but that was a time when I was really only just discovering my sexuality anyway.

Did you know you were gay before you began your training?
I have always felt 'different' even from an early age — not enjoying all the things boys are supposed to do, particularly sport, mainly football which I loathe. I was always teased because of this. I don't consider that I was effeminate, but perhaps 'soft', oversensitive, innocent.

As a teenager I was a late developer, though not the latest, but never really got into girlfriends — not that I wasn't interested or that I didn't think about marriage and family life, I just didn't ever feel any inclination towards girlfriends as others do. I did have one or two good female friends and used to think that perhaps one day... but we never got as far as kissing even.

When I was 24 I made friends with a priest who helped me a great deal and really introduced me to hugging and touching friends. I had been frightened to get close to any adult until then. This led on to kissing — I had never kissed anyone, let alone a man, a priest even worse still! He was older, bigger, stronger and yet I trusted him — he helped me in many ways. Our sexual activity was very limited, mutual masturbation. I still didn't really regard myself as homosexual and thought of it as a sexual awakening in safe hands.

What effect did your time at seminary have on your understanding and acceptance of your sexuality?
When I went to the seminary and was asked about sexual activity during the selection process I said there had been none, I didn't think they would be too impressed at what had happened. In my first year one of my fellow students told me he was attracted to me — I was feeling disheartened about masturbation, but he said he would like to start a relationship with me. It all began very innocently (at least on my part) but he was calculating and knew exactly what he wanted. He very much took control whilst I was 'so in love'. Eventually after a year of mutual masturbation our relationship developed to include anal intercourse, though always with a condom. Then I realized that yes, I definitely was homosexual — nothing felt wrong about the sexual activity, but there was much guilt about it having to take place so secretly, in private, with no opportunity to talk about it freely and openly. (Also about the celibacy problem.) I dare not talk about this with my spiritual director as my lover was a fellow student so talked to another priest outside the seminary — he told me to run away from the situation. Even in my naïvety I realized that I must deal with it head on: being (1) called to the priesthood and celibacy,

and (2) homosexual.

Unbeknown to me, my lover had been making sexual advances to quite a lot of the other students — some had obliged, others had complained. Eventually he was asked to leave which totally devastated me — I could no longer talk about it with anyone else and felt more and more guilty. On a couple of occasions I took 'comfort' with a mutual friend, but he too really took advantage. I suffered from depression and eventually confided in my spiritual director who had guessed the problem anyway. He was very supportive, though not homosexual himself. It was a great weight lifted off my shoulders in that he accepted me and treated me lovingly. After that I wanted to shout it off the rooftops but thankfully I didn't. My depression was to continue and eventually my spiritual director put me in touch with a psychologist (at my request) who helped me a great deal with problems wider than just the sexuality, though this was probably the major concern of mine. The psychologist helped me to put my sexuality into a context which helped me to accept and love myself — hence my present-day position.

One major blow came two years ago when a member of staff [at the seminary] very badly handled a situation and encouraged me to tell him all — he breached my trust and everything went to the rector and bishop. My future was in the balance and the bishop supported me and told me it didn't matter, because I had taken steps to help myself.

Was the issue of homosexuality among the clergy dealt with at seminary? If so, how?
Homosexuality was only covered in moral theology and not particularly well. Homosexuality among the clergy was never mentioned apart from an unconventional member of staff in my final year, but albeit briefly and inadequately.

How comfortable are you with the discipline of celibacy?
I am happy to remain celibate — life is less complicated that way. I feel it would be difficult to sustain a single relationship with the pressures, stresses and strains of pastoral ministry.

If you are sexually active does this have any effect on your wider ministry as a priest? Do you feel guilty about this?
If you are not sexually active does this have any effect on your wider ministry as a priest?
What helps you to remain celibate?

I do masturbate from time to time and sometimes I feel guilty about this, other times I am more realistic. I don't think masturbation is a necessary aid to celibacy — it is at my weaker moments that I succumb. I have made vows at diaconate and priestly ordination to remain celibate — these I hope to fulfil with God's help although I realize that I may fail in the future. So far I haven't — despite the passes of older priests!

What support networks do you find helpful?
In seminary, my spiritual director and my psychologist and after the problems encountered three members of staff were supportive at that time. Also personal friends, including some of my fellow seminarians — very few of these people homosexual themselves.

Does your bishop/superior know that you are gay?
As a gay priest do you think you can count on the support of your bishop/superior?
As a result of problems bishop now knows and is supportive — but I am lucky with my bishop. With a different bishop things would not be the same.

Are you involved with Justice and Peace work as part of your ministry? Do you think that the Church should be concerned with the rights of lesbian and gay people as a justice issue or are you more comfortable with homosexuality being seen as a moral issue?
I feel marginalized as must do coloured people, handicapped people and other groups but there is a danger of a ghetto mentality — I believe in integration of individual people within the Christian family, whatever their label. I do feel injustice towards homosexuals, but that is by our homophobic society, particularly the media. I think that AIDS has helped the Church to look on homosexuality from a pastoral (therefore J&P) point of view, rather than a moral dilemma.

What do you like most about being a priest?
Pastoral concerns, celebrating mass and particularly the sacrament of reconciliation.

What do you like least about being a priest?
Pressures of life, tension, stress, tiredness. Need to keep quiet about my inclination — but that is not limited to priesthood.

What advice would you give to a gay student for the priesthood?
You must talk to someone you trust — and not someone you are sexually involved with. Someone who will help you to face the issue

rather than run away from it. Take care who you trust and pray about it before you do so. Trust is very important. 'Do not worry about tomorrow.' Be proud of who you are and your mistakes — they are part of you, your make-up and history — we learn from life's experiences, good and bad. Don't become bitter; don't become a jealous old queen. They say 'Hell hath no fury like a woman scorned' — homosexuals can be worse. Don't associate with all-homosexual groups, particularly in seminary — they get a reputation it may be hard to live down.

Take care of yourself. 'You are precious in my eyes, I am your father and I love you with a perfect love.' Living a double life will take its toll and break you in the end. When I was 'outed' at seminary, although very distressing and humiliating it was also liberating and freeing. I no longer had to look over my shoulder which was a great relief.

Father David

In many ways I am not happy with the questionnaire that I received. I suppose I am still not as integrated as I want to be as an individual, as a Catholic, or as a gay person. Watching what has been happening in the Protestant Churches I am not over-enthusiastic to be speaking anonymously about my sexual orientation in connection with my commitment to priesthood. I know that in many people's eyes — and I include other gay eyes — when they hear that a priest is gay they immediately presume promiscuous behaviour and bar-hopping. I can definitely state that I know many good priests and some of these are gay — my own admiration for the work of these priests far excels any knowledge that I have of their misgivings or failures. I certainly don't want to be one of those individuals who spends a great deal of time knocking the priesthood or using its failures to support other agendas.

If I were to tell you that the most difficult part of my life was admitting to myself that I was gay, then I hope you will understand what follows. I was always taught that being gay was something peculiar and unnatural. One of my cousins was gay and my mother used to warn us about him and my relatives used to joke and make fun of him. Actually he was always pleasant enough to me but I never wanted to know him and I avoided his company and that of his friends. I suppose I spent most of my life joining in the classic witch-hunts and denigrating characters who were effeminate and 'poofs' or 'queers'. Clerical conversation often homes in on characters that are different and it is the easiest label to call someone gay or lesbian — and by God, it sticks.

When I finally came to realize that I was in love with someone of my own sex, I had been ordained 5 years and it was an experience that tore me apart. I left the priesthood eventually for a year and returned (hopefully) having sorted myself out and enjoying the realization that I could be both gay and priest.

It was then that I realized how much the official Church is afraid of homosexuality. Priests talking about refusing ministry to gay men and AIDS used as an excuse for not giving the chalice to the faithful enraged me. I began to be involved with hospice ministry and found not only that I enjoyed the company of other gay men but that I began to listen very seriously to their faith needs and how neglected they felt in the Catholic Church. I was impressed with ministers from the Anglican religion who seemed very open and happier in many ways. I have always been surprised at the number of closet cases that there are among the clergy and even more surprised at their homophobia. Sisters are just as just as bad when it comes to homophobia — they can't all be lesbians, although I have a feeling quite a few are on the border.

I am not happy being unable to tell my family or my bishop that I am gay; although I am happy being gay. Other gay men have a way of understanding that is to their credit and I find this unspoken bond a great help to me.

Perhaps in my heart I wish the Church could be more receptive and tolerant and be as prepared to learn as I have found most gay men. I'm convinced that fear is the key to this — and I believe that my own orientation has helped me to identify many areas of Church life that I disagree with and can openly work towards changing. I believe the Catholic Church will also make its way very slowly to a renewed morality which will be far more inclusive and broadminded than at present and realize the treasures that have been neglected so long with regard to many areas of orientation and life-style.

I believe the faithful themselves have taken a great lead in refusing to kowtow to mindless homophobia such as Cardinal Ratzinger presents. The health crisis around the world has not seen the involvement of the Catholic Church and the faithful themselves can see this. The platitudes of prelates and old dictators will be met with the same response as the people of Eastern Europe gave their unelected masters. And the more say that the laity are given in the running of the Church the less emphasis there will be on depreciating sex and looking at it all as filth rather than God-given.

Gay men have long memories and will remember those who came

to their assistance and those who were the first to cast stones! The growth of the Metropolitan Community Church [a Church founded in 1968 in the United States for lesbian and gay people. It is now one of the fastest growing Christian denominations] is witness to the outrageous treatment so many have received.

I'm a strange mixture of not wanting to criticize and yet needing to be angry about so many things and not all of them to do with the Church. Society/government/the system is as much to blame for the way gay men are treated and I personally would like to get more involved in changing the legal status of homosexuals. This to me is to do with natural justice and I'm annoyed that with so many gay MPs and gay juridical individuals that so little has been done.

And it is the same with the clergy — so many gay clergy and so little done to support and encourage, affirm and bring about the changes that would make so much difference to the Church.

And LGCM? I'm not sure if Catholics needed a gay Caucus when they do have Quest — an organization that at least tries to work within the company of other Catholics. I'm wondering what the next headline will be — GAY PRIESTS SPEAK OUT — I would like to see something more pastoral being done for all the clergy whatever their orientation.

Father Mark

I am aware that perhaps you expected me to write at greater length and I am happy to do so but found the whole question disturbing. I think it is because it is something that I need to do something about and manage to cope with life if I do not think too much about it. But it's always there waiting for my attention. You see, I thought like many others that gayness would just go away and leave me free to get on with whatever needed to be done. Actually try not dealing with it — it gets worse!

However I do not think that we are different from other people in our sexual desire — just that at the moment it cannot be satisfactorily integrated because of my history and those things were not discussed and sexuality was considered something the animals did or 'other' people — not us! Had I known the difficulties I wonder if I would have sought ordination — possibly subconsciously it may have been why I sought it, i.e. I could not find satisfactory relationships with people so in my need I found God!

I deal with several young men who are coming to grips with their sexuality and a good number are gay or think they are. Some really pray and want to follow the teaching of the Church but I have every sympathy with them when they consider that they may not have the gift of celibacy yet are condemned to live a celibate life. I rather envy those priests who seem to have everything worked out — emotionally and sexually — but do they? Perhaps we are all broken in some way and it is through our brokenness that we are going to find the Lord.

But I must confess and say that if I found a partner who loved me as I loved him I think I would have to think long and deeply but I think I would set up house if possible — but again what can a priest offer in ways of commitment and stability — very little. I wish I had thought about this before I was a priest. But I am a priest and probably will remain one for there is nowhere else to go. I hate being told that I am objectively disordered. I find it depressing. I wish I knew what to do. I know that we have to take up our Cross and follow Jesus. But this Cross hurts deeply and I need love personally — not in a general way but intimate and accepting.

Father Simon

Are you happy to be gay?
Yes. But getting here was not easy. Until about five or six years ago I was vis-à-vis my sexuality what I believe psychiatry calls 'dystonic'. Simply put, I didn't like myself very much. I was in a state of almost constant internal strife. I was gay and a priest! An impossible combination. That was what I heard from Church and society for most of my life. I knew when I was in my early teens that I was gay. In a small town in a remote part of the British Isles my sexuality made me an inferior outsider. A solitary life became more solitary. I had a terrible secret that I could not share with anyone. I simply could not cope with the feared rejection. I didn't want to be a leper. So I pretended. The real me was buried, repressed and oppressed. I interiorized my oppression. May God grant healing to those who suffered as a consequence. The story of my last ten years has been a story of gradually emerging from my self-imposed entombment ... But that too has been achieved not without considerable cost and many mistakes.

What is your view of the Church's teaching on homosexuality?
I believe that there is a growing perception that there is something awry with the Church's teaching on sexuality, period. It is not just an unhappiness shared by homosexual persons. There are signs of a shift occurring in the *sensus fidelium* with regard to this whole area ... Can you imagine Jesus saying to one of his brothers 'You are intrinsically disordered'? ... Every human person is a unique image of God. I wish Church bureaucrats, especially those who lay burdens on people's shoulders, would take this into their heads and hearts.

How did you react to the 1986 Letter on the Pastoral Care of Homosexual Persons?

Cardinal Ratzinger's 1986 letter I found unhelpful. It caused a lot of good Christians to feel hurt and marginalized. It contained a shocking statement: 'When civil legislation is introduced to protect behaviour to which no one has any right, neither the Church nor society should be surprised when other distorted notions and practices gain ground, and irrational and violent reactions increase.' ...

Did it change your behaviour and attitudes in any way?

I suspect that the principal effect Ratzinger's letter had on me was to make me more radically aligned with those who felt oppressed by it.

Did you know you were gay before you began your training?
What effect did your time at seminary have on your understanding and acceptance of your sexuality?
Was the issue of homosexuality among the clergy dealt with at seminary? If so, how?

I fell in love for the first time at seminary. This was an entirely emotional/platonic affair. Apart from this the seminary was not a helpful place for befriending sexuality. What is rather sad is that there was, in my experience, a total lack of any kind of realistic treatment of the candidate for orders as a sexual being. This was simply not addressed. Homosexuality was a taboo subject. It was dealt with only by the phenomenon of people (by the pair) disappearing mysteriously and without official comment from the seminary-scape.

How comfortable are you with the discipline of celibacy?

I thought I was reasonably comfortable with [celibacy], but I suspect I have been deluding myself. When I set out to celebrate my life in ministry I was happy to embrace this discipline. As with marriage there are three parties to the deal: God, the Candidate and the Church. However, apart from her requirement of celibacy, the Church does not really do much to support the priest who has submitted to and embraced the discipline. Increasingly, with the shrinkage of priestly resources, we are burdened with loneliness. And I do not mean just the loneliness of being alone. That is bad enough. But it can be almost intolerable when it is compounded by loneliness of vision and spirituality. I am, at the time of writing, looking after a small community on a temporary basis. A member of this community said to me recently, 'I wish you could stay with us.

As you well know there are not many spiritual priests around.' It was a comment that I found both profoundly affirming and moving but one which also made me feel very sad.

A man who embraces celibacy renounces biological generativity. I believe that it is imperative for those who hold positions of management in the Church to ensure that a man's generativity can be expressed in other ways. This, in my opinion, is essential in the early years of a young man's ministry. All too easily a person's giftedness, creativity and vision can at best be ignored or at worst ridiculed. I am not talking 'carte blanche', but healthy enablement. All too often the Church simply treats her priests as pawns on a chessboard. I have been through seven major moves and twice been on temporary supply since my ordination. I have never been left anywhere for more than three years. It saddens me that there seems to be little appreciation, on the part of our managers, of the psychic and spiritual toll this exacts.

If you are sexually active does this have any effect on your wider ministry as a priest? Do you feel guilty about this?
If you are not sexually active does this have any effect on your wider ministry as a priest?
What helps you to remain celibate?
I used to have terrible guilt problems but not any more. The guilt was more associated with 'being homosexual and a priest' than anything else. I have put more energy into sustaining celibacy than undermining it. When I have been in a committed relationship with another person that has had no negative effect on my ministry.

Does your being gay affect your relationship with other clergy?
Without doubt, but in largely unconscious ways I suspect. Or at least that was the case until fairly recently. At this moment in time I really do not know where I stand in the affections of my diocesan colleagues. I have been told that they are angry with me as a consequence of an indiscretion that resulted in my victimization and scapegoating. Meanwhile I am in voluntary exile.

What support networks do you find helpful?
My family, my close friends — and my psychotherapist!

Does your bishop/superior know that you are gay?
Yes. The fact that I am a gay man is widely known.

As a gay priest do you think you can count on the support of your bishop/superior?

[I can count on the support of my bishop] as a celibate gay priest. He has no other choice.

Are you involved with Justice and Peace work as part of your ministry? Do you think that the Church should be concerned with the rights of lesbian and gay people as a justice issue or are you more comfortable with homosexuality being seen as a moral issue?

Justice is a high priority on my agenda. It is one of the signs of hope abroad that there is in our society today a growing hunger for deeper social and ecological justice. But our society must be careful to ensure that it is not selective in its pursuit of this justice. When confronted with questions of justice the Christian gospel does not allow silence. Christians have to be deeply invested in the pursuit of justice and that justice is indivisible. The 13th-century Dominican mystic and theologian Meister Eckhart has this to say: 'People who love justice will be admitted to justice, seized by justice, and one with justice. A just person is one who is conformed and transformed into justice. The just person is like God, for God is justice. Whoever resides in justice resides in God and is God.' . . .

However, it has to be acknowledged that the institutional Church has not always enfleshed the gospel's call to justice in its relations with minority groups in its midst, be they Jews, Muslims, homosexual persons, or native peoples. It has been silent while the earth has been ravished by man's selfish ruthlessness . . .

We must all listen with respect to the voices of those who are marginalized and hurting. Homosexuality undoubtedly demands consideration as a justice issue before one even begins to reflect on the moral issues. Gay and lesbian people are often discriminated against on the grounds of their sexuality. Homophobia is the main culprit here. Homophobia is evil and the Church must both name it and ensure that she is not also driven by it.

What do you like most about being a priest?

Preaching the gospel, the empowering and enabling of people to live a liberated life in Christ, and celebration of the liturgy.

What do you like least about being a priest?

The 'pedestal syndrome' (the habit people have of putting priests on pedestals), administration, building management and maintenance, and endless meetings — especially those involving other clergy!

Are you involved with the 'out' gay community at all?

I am a member of the Lesbian and Gay Christian Movement and assist my local [gay] community organization.

Do you think it would be helpful to you/other gay or lesbian Catholics if there were more 'out' gay people in the local Church community?
Yes.

Have you had any particularly positive or negative experiences in the Church as a result of your sexuality?
In my recent past I fell victim to the indiscretion mentioned above. That has resulted in what I can only call a very public crucifixion. I was stripped of my good name, reputation and ministry. This was accomplished by evil persons who wove a convincing tapestry of half-truth and untruth. Their object was to 'out' me. There was financial advantage for them in doing so. What grieved me most was that it was through their wretched efforts that my mother discovered the truth about my sexuality. It was also the way in which the wider Church and world learnt about it. This has possibly been the most negative and traumatic event of my life. It could also have been terminally crippling.

What was achieved was the public humiliation of my family, my former parishioners and myself. That humiliation was achieved by the demon of homophobia ... We are left in no doubt about the very real hostile attitude to gay people manifested by certain of this country's tabloid newspapers. It is an attitude that is quite shocking in its lack of humanity, decency and appalling generalizations. Such homophobia must be named for what it is, evil. There is another aspect of this that needs to be addressed. It has to do with the dominant patriarchy of our culture and with abuse of male power. It is about aggressiveness that takes advantage of and abuses the vulnerability of the weak and powerless. The late Richie J. McMullin in *Male Rape* (1990) makes the insightful comment, 'School bullies and those who attack minority group members rarely attack those capable of defending themselves adequately. This abuse of power is almost daily evidenced in the "gutter" press.' This does not reflect well on either the press or our society. As I remarked earlier, the Christian Church too has to accept a considerable amount of responsibility for creating the context out of which homophobia emerges and in which it often continues to seek to justify itself.

As awful as my experience has been I have to say that a great deal of good has emerged from it. And believe me it has been a real dark night time. I have been exiled from my good name, reputation, diocese and ministry. But in the midst of all this I have come home, as never before, to my real self. I have become more integrally individuated, more deeply rooted in myself, in my family, and my Creator and Sustainer. They, and my friends, have put a fortress of love about me.

Is there anything you know now that you wish you'd known before you were ordained?
I wish I had had the opportunity to know other gay and lesbian people and to realize how 'normal' I really was. Though that knowledge could possibly have altered my vocational choice.

What advice would you give to a gay student for the priesthood?
Think very carefully and long before you commit yourself and be sure that you know and love yourself. Know that you are a unique image of God. There never has been and there never will be again an image of God like you. When Jesus walked on water towards his disciples (Mark 6:50) he says to them, 'Take heart! It is I! Do not be afraid.' Keep these words before you each day. Stay close to Jesus who is close to you and have courage. And for those dark winter nights of the soul keep in mind and heart these words of Mother Julian of Norwich, 'winter will come and pass and all will be well'.

Be aware that the present organization of the priestly ministry in the institution may not really give the adequate support that is needed for living a celibate life-style. You will need to rely on your own resources. You will need to cultivate a deep and faithful prayer life and great generosity of heart. The American counselling guru John Egan once visited my seminary. Of the many things he said all I can remember is the following: 'Marriage and celibacy are complementary. Those in the married state are called to give witness to the depth of God's love. Those who are celibate are called to give witness to the breadth of God's love.' So strive for and live great generosity of heart.

If you really feel and believe you cannot respond to the demand of celibacy and envisage some kind of active sexual life be sure that you can live with the tensions that will involve. Make sure you have a spiritual director or soul friend. Be all the more certain that you truly know yourself. Try and avoid the commercial 'scene'. It is a potentially dangerous place. Join the Lesbian and Gay Christian Movement.

Thomas, a seminarian

Are you happy to be gay?
Yes.

What is your view of the Church's teaching on homosexuality?
I apply it creatively.

How did you react to the 1986 Letter on the Pastoral Care of Homosexual Persons?
Anger, coupled with objective rejection.

Did it change your behaviour and attitudes in any way?
No, except that my conviction was affirmed that Rome wants to inflict a homophobic backlash to gay liberation. I reject a rigid application of Catholic sexual ethics as in fact very unCatholic: for in my reading of Catholic morality there are principles and there are people whose lives are to be served by and not dictated to by those principles. All principles have to be creatively applied to our present lived realities, for God takes us as we are and so must we. God is always alongside us in all we do, encouraging us towards wholeness. If for any of us at this time this includes being sexually active then God's fundamental invitation to us is to be true to ourselves, to take risks *for* life, to be responsible in all we do and loving in all we are.

In its present expression, Catholic morality on gay life-style is simply saying that our community is fundamentally oriented towards male–female interplay, which is profoundly reasonable as we are perpetuated by this relationship and indeed families and kids are crucial to parish life. I think this interplay can be a humanizing perspective for gay relationships, exploring the 'male'–'female' interplay in such single-sex relationships and also gay commitments to family/community. Within this context, Catholic morality has developed from a dismissal of homosexuality as perverse; to pretend that we gays remain, in our perceptions, at this level is naïvety and bigotry itself; and sadly, in my view, it is precisely this which now motivates again magisterial pronouncements.

Did you know you were gay before you began your training?
Yes.

What effect did your time at seminary have on your understanding and acceptance of your sexuality?
That there are lots of us about and a number are not permitted to realize who they are.

Was the issue of homosexuality among the clergy dealt with at seminary? If so, how?
Not explicitly, but our course was quite positive.

How comfortable are you with the discipline of celibacy?
Well, I'm just about to freely choose celibacy as a deacon! I am quite uncomfortable about the discipline of celibacy. I do not see its worth and I personally reject its official necessity. As to what it means — I see too many sad clerics to believe it works for many; for some, yes.

I choose celibacy at this time for priesthood and no other reason; yet I also freely choose it, at long last, as a statement that I am no longer hunting for the 'tall, dark stranger' in my life. I am exploring prayer and love of many — i.e. parish communities — instead, and trying to live my loneliness from this perspective, rather than hankering after the 'impossible dream'. After all, marriage is difficult, so is being a bachelor, so is being a celibate (which is NOT about being a bachelor, it's about being a lover!).

If you are sexually active does this have any effect on your wider ministry?
To be more 'feeling' and sensitive to myself and others as a human person.

Do you feel guilty about this?
No.

If you are not sexually active does this have any effect on your wider ministry?
I can become closed in by loneliness (negatively) or more energized to be outwardgoing in loving others (positively).

What helps you to remain celibate?
Receiving love.

Does your being gay affect your relationship with other clergy?
I keep myself to myself, but it's quite easy to be slightly camp with
fellow priests because so many of us are!

What support networks do you find helpful?
My prayer support group (lay), Ministry to Priests.

Does your bishop/superior know that you are gay?
No.

*As a gay priest do you think you can count on the support of your bishop/
superior?*
No — quite the opposite. I would not be ordained I consider.

*Are you involved with Justice and Peace work as part of your ministry? Do
you think that the Church should be concerned with the rights of lesbian
and gay people as a justice issue or are you more comfortable with
homosexuality being seen as a moral issue?*
Yes. Definitely justice.

What do you think you will like most about being a priest?
Being loved and affirmed by so many (experienced as a full-time lay
parish pastoral assistant for 2 years).

What do you think you will like least about being a priest?
Being distanced by others, not treated as a human person.

Are you involved with the 'out' gay community at all?
Yes, Quest at present. Just in London, not my own diocese (yet!).

*Do you think it would be helpful to you/other gay or lesbian Catholics if
there were more 'out' gay people in the local Church community?*
To each other; but we can't walk hand-in-hand in Church yet, that's
unrealistic; but 'singles' carrying out their lay ministries, just being
natural — people can be quite accepting.

*Have you had any particularly positive or negative experiences in the
Church as a result of your sexuality?*
[Positive experiences] Some have welcomed my openness.
[Negative experiences] I've found diocesan selection psychological
tests profoundly disturbing, unfair and hurtful.

What advice would you give to a gay student for the priesthood?
Be true to yourself, but be very careful who you talk to.

Vernon, a seminarian

Are you happy to be gay?
Yes — definitely — happy to be who I am. (Not that I was to begin with. Coming out to myself involved pain etc.)

Did you know you were gay before you began your training?
Yes. Began training at age of 24.

What effect did your time at seminary have on your understanding and acceptance of your sexuality?
So far: none really. Grown in acceptance.

Was the issue of homosexuality among the clergy dealt with at seminary? If so, how?
No. Completely avoided, swept under the carpet and all discussion rejected. Great homophobia in the college. (For me to bring it up would be disastrous.)

How comfortable are you with the discipline of celibacy?
Intellectually I don't find it authentic.

If you are sexually active does this have any effect on your wider ministry? Do you feel guilty about this?
If you are not sexually active does this have any effect on your wider ministry?
What helps you to remain celibate?
Despite expectations of one or two others, I'm not actually looking for sex or a relationship so the question hasn't (yet?) arisen. That's not to say I'd avoid a relationship if it turned up. Saw a glorious and unexpected whirlwind romance the other week and it's continuing well for the future. And without realizing it I set it up!

Does your being gay affect your relationship with other clergy?
Yes it helps — at least with the few I'm 'out' with. As I'm not out to
the rest it doesn't interfere there. Those few I trust.

What support networks do you find helpful?
Regional gay social group.

Does your bishop/superior know that you are gay?
No.

*As a gay priest do you think you can count on the support of your bishop/
superior?*
Bishop yes; seminary rector, probably not.

*Are you involved with Justice and Peace work as part of your ministry? Do
you think that the Church should be concerned with the rights of lesbian
and gay people as a justice issue or are you more comfortable with
homosexuality being seen as a moral issue?*
Will be. It's necessarily both. It shouldn't just be hived off into one
compartment and left there — e.g. given just two lines in the J&P
section of a 2-volume document. It should be dealt with in parishes
where people (especially aged 14–21) are trying to deal with it —
with very little help; help that is badly needed.

What do you think you will like most about being a priest?
Experiencing Christ's love and liberation making sense in my life and
bringing it to others.

What do you think you will like least about being a priest?
Totally unrealistic expectations. Behaviour patterns as conformity to
an institution (or inappropriate behaviour as the lack of it).

Are you involved with the 'out' gay community at all?
Yes, but only just. Coming to it slowly and gradually. Joined regional
group last month aged 27. Support there.

*Do you think it would be helpful to you/other gay or lesbian Catholics if
there were more 'out' gay people in the local Church community?*
Yes — though need to bear in mind misunderstanding, upset and
alienation on *both* sides of the debate.

*Have you had any particularly positive or negative experiences in the
Church as a result of your sexuality?*
[Positive experiences] Only ecumenically or from very few clergy.
[Negative experiences] Plenty. Implicit rejection from frankly bigoted
students in the seminary. Sorry this sounds judgemental. Nothing I

can do about that.

Is there anything you know now that you wish you'd known before you began training?
If I'd known too much before I'd gone away to seminary it would have distracted me or put me off. Better in a way to be thrown in at the deep end, and get on with survival — even swim against the current.

What advice would you give to a gay student for the priesthood?
Stick at it; and find a support group (impossible in the foreign seminaries). We need priests who are gay and happy in our sexuality!

Will, a seminarian

Are you happy to be gay?

If you are asking 'Am I glad to be gay?' then the answer would probably be No. I don't think anyone would choose to be part of a minority with all the problems that entails. Part of me yearns for the life I see others living and which is not possible for me to live (at one time I would have said 'denied to me' but that paints a very odd picture of God my creator). I would love to have a family and I do enjoy the company of children and women. But, as I have always functioned as a gay man, I do not know if it would have been possible to make the commitment required to honestly stay with one other person.

If you are asking 'Are you at home with your sexuality?' then I can be more positive and say generally Yes. This was a long process and it is not yet over. For many years I prayed that I would somehow be made 'normal'. If that was not possible then at least for the switch that made me sexually aroused at the sight of some men to turn to the 'off' position and that I could be neutral! As I see it, sexuality is one of the bits that go to make up the person that is me. However, the bits are fluid and so it is like trying to make a jigsaw with pieces that are constantly changing; just when you think you have one part of the picture in place, everything starts to move apart! I am now happier and at ease with my gayness and accept it as just a part of what it is to be me. It still is the cause of much heartache as well as joy but then the same can be said for any aspect of sexuality.

What is your view of the Church's teaching on homosexuality?
How did you react to the 1986 Letter on the Pastoral Care of Homosexual Persons?

Did it change your behaviour and attitudes in any way?
The 1986 'letter' was not the most supportive piece of writing I have ever read! Like a lot of the Church's moral teaching, I feel that it should carry a 'Health Warning'. They are the results of much learned, if sometimes blinkered, study and should really only be read by moral theologians. They are academic exercises and any findings arrived at are not tempered with pastoral needs. The language used in places was decidedly unhelpful and I think the last hasn't been heard on the subject. Hopefully through books like the one you're preparing it will be possible to temper thoughts of the Curia and create a more enlightened atmosphere of understanding and pastoral concern for gay men and women, both religious and lay. If the Church accepted that a large number of its ministers are gay (as a seminarian, I look at the numbers in my own college as a representative sample) it may not want to change its moral norms but it may well alter its approach to the situation. Many of my thoughts on this issue are reflections of those found in Jeannine Gramick and Pat Furey, *The Vatican and Homosexuality*.

Did you know you were gay before you began your training?
What effect did your time at seminary have on your understanding and acceptance of your sexuality?
Was the issue of homosexuality among the clergy dealt with at seminary? If so, how?
Yes. I feel I have known my orientation since I was 7 and was sexually active, albeit in a furtive way, from the age of 15.

The question of homosexuality is one that has only been dealt with in an oblique way at college. We have had some very sensitive talks and presentations during retreats etc. but it is all a bit hypothetical. There has not been any positive reinforcement and acceptance of the homosexual state and of the caring qualities that some gay people have. Or the fact that, because they are gay, they may feel called to share their lives with many rather than one other person in marriage. Those of us who are (as I said before, it is probably a lot higher than in a representative sample from outside) tend to keep the head down and nose clean. It doesn't pay to camp it up in the cloisters! Not that anyone has ever said that gayness is a bar to ordination but there is the feeling that it would be seen as more serious if a guy was sleeping around with other guys rather than with women. Almost as if it was going to be harder for gays to live a celibate life than straights. Because sexuality is never challenged in a positive way I think there are some students who don't know, or won't admit, whether they're Martha or Arthur and I feel this does not bode well for them in their ministry and later life. If you are going to have a crisis with sexuality then it would be better to have it in the caring community that a seminary should be than out in a parish.

How comfortable are you with the discipline of celibacy?
If you are sexually active does this have any effect on your wider ministry?
Do you feel guilty about this?
If you are not sexually active does this have any effect on your wider ministry?
What helps you to remain celibate?

I can't answer this question as I have not accepted the discipline of celibacy. And, as the poet said, 'You don't know what it's like till you've tried it'. Yes, it is something to which I aspire and once having made the commitment, it is what I will try (with the help of God) to carry out. It is something I have struggled with up to now and, as I will be the same person after ordination as I was before, it is something I will have to struggle with as a priest. I know that I cannot do it on my own. As for guilt: my teachers did a good job on me when I was young but I am getting better!!!

Does your being gay affect your relationship with other clergy?

This has not yet been experienced as seminarians are neither fish nor fowl. On my summer placements I try to behave as honestly as I do with any new group of people. I have had a 'poofter' comment behind my back from one priest in a nearby parish, but my shoulders are not so weak and narrow that I took any notice. Anything else I could say in this area would be speculation. Priests are no better or worse when it comes to acceptance of the problems of others. Each has strengths and weaknesses so I do not envisage it being any different to my life before seminary.

What support networks do you find helpful?

The only support networks I use are from those of my spiritual director, who is also gay, and from those friends, both religious and lay who have known me for many years. My 'coming out' with those people close to me, including my family, was both a joyful and painful experience. Those close to me had known me for more than ten years yet as I felt it, there was the possibility, no matter how small, of rejection. This didn't happen and the relationships both deepened and blossomed. In over half of the cases it wasn't the shock

I thought it would be for them. With the rest, all I received was hugs and much love and acceptance (except from my brother, but that is not relevant here — we've always rowed and this one was mega!). It is so much easier to be in the company of people who love all of you. It was also a growing experience for me in coming to terms with my sexuality. There was still the discipline of being discreet. In one way it was a pity I left it until I was 36 before I had the confidence and the courage to do it. This was at the same time as I was embarking on my only excursion into a long-term relationship with another man. This lasted 18 months and ended with much heartache and animosity.

Does your bishop/superior know that you are gay?
My bishop and rector do not know that I am gay. At least they have not asked me and I haven't told them. At my interview with the Bishop I was asked questions that I could answer honestly without telling the whole story. 'What about marriage and relationships?' I was able to tell him that I had been involved in relationships that had led me to accept that marriage wasn't for me. There was one long relationship with a woman from college, when I was training to be a teacher, that was sexual but only at the heavy groping level. If I had been asked 'Are you gay?' at the interview, I can honestly say I don't know how I would have answered. Part of me would have been happy to lie about it but most of me would have wanted to be honest, regardless of the consequences.

As a gay priest do you think you can count on the support of your bishop/ superior?
I am almost certain that I cannot rely on the support of the Bishop. This is based upon listening to the opinions of others in my diocese. I know that other students/priests from other dioceses have the full support of their bishop as to their sexuality (not to the active expression in a relationship). If the subject came up in interview with my rector I think I would feel able to be honest with him. He has known me for several years and is a good judge of character as well as having a sound pastoral outlook.

Are you involved with Justice and Peace work as part of your ministry? Do you think that the Church should be concerned with the rights of lesbian and gay people as a justice issue or are you more comfortable with homosexuality being seen as a moral issue?
I am not involved in J&P at college but see it as an area that should be encouraged at parish level. As to homosexuality being a moral or a

justice issue I would wobble firmly in the middle and say both/and rather than either/or. If you want me to come off the fence then probably at the present time I am happier with it as a moral issue but do not rule out a change of emphasis in the future. (These wishy-washy liberals are all the same!)

Are you involved with the 'out' gay community at all?
I am not involved with any kind of 'out' gay work. My feelings as to 'outing' are still very mixed. I have said how much I was able to grow when I chose to come out with those close to me. However, I also feel that, in one sense, coming out is really a form of going in. Outing of itself does not bring about the changes in attitude that it desires in the 'straight' community. I think it is too closely connected to extremes and to politics. The only good to come out of the 'outing' campaign in summer 1991 was to expose the hypocrisy of the press.

Do you think it would be helpful to you/other gay or lesbian Catholics if there were more 'out' gay people in the local Church community?
In the light of the above answer it may seem strange to say 'yes'.

Have you had any particularly positive or negative experiences in the Church as a result of your sexuality?
I can illustrate both aspects of this question by reference to two incidents involving relationships with clergy. Whilst on my first visit to Rome I went to confession in St Peter's. It was in the 'box' (not my choice of venue) but after telling of a brief 'encounter' with an old friend who I had not seen for years, the priest refused absolution! He then went on to tell me that I had no right even thinking of presenting myself for priesthood and should go back to my college, tell the rector and leave! This is not what I needed to hear. After making subsequent enquiries I learnt that he was notorious and rarely gave absolution for anything! The visit ended on a positive note when I spent a wonderful half-hour walking around the Piazza Navona with a priest I hardly knew, being accepted and cared for and finally absolved.

The real start to my growth as a balanced 'gay' Catholic came about after the break up of the affair I mentioned earlier. The local assistant priest and I were talking over the trauma of the relationship and at one point I said 'I am gay'. He replied, 'No. You are Will.' It was not really until that time could I make the distinction between my manhood and my gayness. Till then, I had seen my whole self through the eyes of my sexuality. I can now see that I am first and foremost a creation of God, loved by him and precious in his eyes, and one part of me (even though it is a very vital part) is gay.

Is there anything you know now that you wish you'd known before you began training?
I am glad that this kind of discussion is going on now and that these questions are being asked before I am (God willing) ordained.

What advice would you give to a gay student for the priesthood?
As a gay student for the priesthood I would encourage any other student who felt called by God to serve in this particular way. On the occasions when I have spoken with fellow students in my own and other seminaries I have tried to help them see their sexuality in the wider context of them as a person. When asked if they should leave because they have discovered their orientation or because they are having difficulty with relationships I have offered them all I have: time and space and a reasonable pair of ears.

'Not a helpful place'
The gay man and the seminary

The priests and seminarians were asked whether they knew they were gay before beginning their training at seminary. They were asked what effect their time at seminary had upon their understanding and acceptance of their sexuality and whether the subject was dealt with at seminary and, if so, how. Four of the respondents did not know that they were gay before beginning their training for the priesthood. This reflects the conclusions reached by James Wolf in his survey of gay priests in the United States. He discovered that 75.2 per cent of his sample knew they were gay before they entered seminary (*Gay Priests*, p. 34). Although he had always felt 'different' and had already had a homosexual relationship before he entered seminary Brian only fully accepted his homosexuality at seminary when he fell in love with a fellow student. One of the priests in our survey explains why he did not realize his sexual orientation until after entering seminary: 'I trained in the 1950s when only very, very limited references were made to homosexuality.' Another wrote:

> I did not know I was gay when I was ordained. I knew I was not attracted to women but that is not the same thing. The issue was not really spoken about as it was assumed we had already come to a conclusion.

Looking back on their decision to offer themselves for training for the priesthood or religious life, a few priests, among them Mark, believe that they were unconsciously or consciously looking for a way to channel their sexuality:

> I suppose that I knew I was gay from earlier teenage years, although I was not quite sure what it was. It was at age 25 that I

started to 'try my vocation' and looking back I think that wanting to be a priest was a way of coping with my sexuality. That said, I am sure that God leads through all our mixed motives, to priesthood or whatever.

I had some inkling that I was gay before I started training for the priesthood. My first sex experience was when I was aged 10 years. Whilst at school I had several adventures with other boys of my age. On leaving school at 15 years of age I thought I would have a girlfriend and indeed over the next seven years had a string of them. I enjoyed their company but on looking back can see that I did not feel quite the same attraction towards them as I did towards members of my own sex. I certainly never felt any sexual attraction. From 16 to 21 I never had a sexual relationship with another person. Though I was very attracted to several of my close male friends I never got involved sexually with them. I tried to live a good pure Catholic life. When I started training for the priest-hood I thought by becoming a priest I would be able to totally sublimate my sexuality in the service of Christ.

Once at seminary the respondents appear to have had diverse experiences of the way the topic of homosexuality was handled in an academic and non-academic setting. For many, as for Brian and Simon, 'the seminary was not a helpful place for befriending sexuality'.

I knew I was gay before beginning training, but at that time the emphasis was on celibacy not orientation, and so I easily kept it to myself. The seminary at the time I was there (not in this country) was concerned to resist Vatican II and so did not have much time for human matters. Sexuality of any sort among the clergy was not dealt with. (I should say, in deference to the seminary system, that the one I attended was an extreme example and probably did not resemble any others.)

I effectively 'buried' or at least shelved my sexuality during the six years of seminary training, accepting the view that homosexuality was some kind of disease or abnormality. In seminary years I led a celibate life although there were strong emotional attachments to a number of fellow students.

The subject of homosexuality among clergy was merely touched upon. The impression might have been gained that it did not exist.

I did know [I was gay] before training, and was rather terrified when dealing with the subject in moral theology, and the talk by the rector on particular friendships. He for some reason spoke quite often about it! It was embarrassing for me and one or two others who were gay.

In seminary sexuality was never discussed. If anything my time at seminary made me more insecure about myself and my sexuality. It became something to be hidden, not really spoken about except through innuendo. I would estimate that about 20 per cent of my class of thirty were and are gay. The majority would never admit it to themselves let alone anyone else. It would be hinted at and there would be much suggestive talk but that would be all. Homosexuality among the clergy was never spoken about, sexuality wasn't. Formation for celibacy was virtually non-existent.

When I started training for the priesthood I thought by becoming a priest I would be able to totally sublimate my sexuality in the service of Christ. My eight years of training, however, showed me that I could not keep such an important element of my life 'under wraps' and indeed towards the end of my second year of training I fell deeply in love for the first time with another student, and this relationship continued on and off for the next 11 years. This caused us both heartache as we desperately wanted to do what is right and found ourselves often at odds, as I was the more sexually active of the two of us, and we tried long periods of abstinence. I did not feel confident in discussing this with my spiritual director, as I very much wanted to be a priest. If the truth had been known I think I am sure that I would have been asked to leave. I think at ordination I had a very undeveloped attitude to sexuality and was very confused and muddled. The subject of homosexuality was never mentioned once during my training and if it was referred to it was always in the smutty jokes and asides.

I realized I was homosexually inclined in my teenage years but did not become gay until well into my priestly training. I make a distinction between 'gay' and 'homosexual' because, for me, the former implies a healthy acceptance of oneself without guilt. At no point in my training did my religious superiors address the issue of homosexuality. My academic training dealt with it only as a moral theology issue. My own personal acceptance of it came through my spiritual director and my own questioning.

There was a very gay set at [that seminary]. [It was] taken for granted.

[At seminary I had] a gradual growing awareness that I was probably bisexual. The issue was never dealt with at seminary, but neither was heterosexuality. Sex and the priest was never mentioned.

[The seminary had an] essentially good [effect], despite 'the system'. [The issue of homosexuality among the clergy was dealt with] but badly — by a rector who found the whole issue distasteful.

Homosexuality was never dealt with. I never found there were any workshops or discussions. At that stage in my personal development I would not have felt able to bring it up. I suppose you take what is given to you.

The overwhelming agreement amongst these priests is that the subject of homosexuality was not well handled at their seminaries. Some went through seminary without the subject being mentioned except in the context of jokes. Some found it dealt with only in the context of moral theology, that is, within their academic study of Church teaching and its application. Very few had it mentioned within the context of their own formation as priests or religious. Some experienced it within the context of a talk by the rector which was not at all helpful. Wolf discovered that half of his sample of American gay priests thought that the seminary had had a negative influence upon their sexual attitudes, one quarter believed it had had a neutral influence and less than a quarter believed it had some sort of positive influence (*Gay Priests*, p. 35). Our sample is more negative: only one priest believes his seminary experience was essentially good with regards to sexuality. Most believe it had a negative or neutral influence.

What is most surprising, not to say alarming, is that the bad handling of the issue of homosexuality in seminaries is not a problem of the past. Recently ordained priests and seminarians found the same silence or reluctant, purely academic, treatment of homosexuality. As Vernon notes, in his experience the topic of homosexuality in the clergy is 'avoided' and 'swept under the carpet'.

This is surprising considering the trouble to which many seminaries now go to vet candidates before entrance, using psychological tests which do focus at least in part on the candidates' sexuality. It is also now common practice for seminaries to run human-development programmes drawn up with the aid of psychologists and counsellors which are in principle designed to help students reflect upon sexuality, relationships, love, friendship and so on. But although the seminarian respondents have the apparent advantage over their older colleagues in having these programmes designed for them, none finds them helpful with regard to their homosexuality. Gay clergy do not seem to be getting the necessary sex education or formation that Pope John Paul regards as essential.

Men are entering seminary with a diverse experience of being gay. Some have long known and accepted their sexuality; others are only just beginning to realize their sexual orientation; others know and hate their homosexuality; some have had sexual relationships. What all these men have in common is having a sexuality which is at best an embarrassment, at worst unacceptable, to their superiors and fellow students. The natural reaction for both students and teachers in the present Church atmosphere is to try and keep their heads down on this issue. But as the present celibacy crisis in the Church has demonstrated, failing to give seminarians proper education and opportunities for personal formation in the area of sexuality can cause untold harm in the man's future ministry. The first step the Church needs to take in facing up to the reality of gay priests is to recognize the needs of gay seminarians.

Proper sexual and emotional formation can only be built on honesty and mutual trust. Breaches of confidentiality by staff such as Brian experienced and an atmosphere of fear and secrecy surrounding homosexuality prevent seminaries becoming safe and nurturing for gay students. As Sipe has noted 'secrecy obliterates accountability' (*A Secret World*, p. 113). Seminaries must be accountable for their gay students and that means acknowledging their existence and seeking to address their situation. Seminaries and religious orders and congregations need to address the whole issue of gay candidates and students openly and honestly, listening to the experiences of those who have already gone through the system as gay men and, in the spirit of *Pastores Dabo Vobis*, taking into account the latest and best writings on homosexuality produced by the human sciences and theologians, as well as the Vatican's teaching. The purpose of this process would be to draw up a written policy on gay candidates and what gay students can expect in terms of formation and support in the seminary as well as the standards of conduct that would be expected of these men. Prospective candidates have a right to know if being gay will be in itself an obstacle to acceptance or whether a particular attitude to homosexuality is unacceptable. Studying homosexuality only as part of moral theology is simply inadequate as far as gay students are concerned. There are particular problems faced by gay seminarians that have to be faced and dealt with sensitively: a gay priest has to serve and represent an institution which regards their sexuality as disordered; a gay priest living in an institution dominated by men will face different challenges to his sexuality than those experienced by his heterosexual brothers; and there is always the issue of self-acceptance in a society and in a Church riddled with homophobia. This honesty and sensitivity should begin with the vocation director. Basil Pennington, an experienced director of novices, explains why it is so important that gay candidates for the priesthood or religious life should be given a 'safe' opportunity to discuss their sexual orientation at the earliest possible moment.

For one who is opting for celibacy for the Kingdom, in a certain sense it matters little if he be homosexual or heterosexual. What is important is that he have a mature grasp of his sexuality, know his orientation, and fully accept himself and his sexuality as something good. If this is lacking he can never really give himself in love to God nor to anyone else. If he cannot accept himself, he cannot accept the fact that God or anyone else really accepts and loves him. This can be very difficult for a gay person. His self-image is often very poor indeed. The message he has received from society, from his Church, and frequently even from his own parents and family is that he or at least his gayness is bad. A lack of self-acceptance and an inability to accept true affirming love are, I think, the greatest obstacles I run into in regard to gay candidates. ... The vocation father can play a very decisive role in developing this maturity, especially if he is the first straight or first significant person to whom the candidate has revealed his gayness, or the first who fully accepts him with his gayness revealed. The vocation father's full acceptance, with respect and affection, with the assurance that one's sexual orientation is not a bar to his being accepted as a brother, can help the gay man to accept himself as equal to the straight man, as fully acceptable as the straight man ... With great patience and tact the vocation father has to help the candidate to see where the community stands. He has to see if the candidate can really accept this — compassionately accept the limitations and prejudices of the members and live peacefully with them. (M. Basil Pennington, 'Vocation Discernment and the Homosexual' in Robert Nugent, *A Challenge to Love*, pp. 241–2)

Of course, the vocation director himself will have to be aware and accepting of his own sexual orientation, whatever it may be, in order to be able to discuss honestly, openly and creatively such issues with candidates. It must also be remembered that seminaries and religious congregations are not places where candidates are supposed to arrive perfected. They are places of growth and formation and whilst in the present climate it may be advisable (but against the official practice in many cases) only to admit candidates who know and accept their sexuality, ideally these institutions should be able to welcome wounded and self-doubting men and nurture them into self-love.

Whilst few would doubt the wisdom of devising well-researched and conducted screening procedures to test the call of the candidate, assess his mental and physical health and pinpoint areas of his life and personality which will need to be worked on, there is a widespread belief that some of these tests are designed to weed out gay men. If that is the case then this must be acknowledged honestly and justified. If the intention is simply to weed out a certain type of gay man, this also needs to be acknowledged. Otherwise, justice demands that gay and straight candidates should be treated equally in the screening process. Since most psychologists now acknowledge that gay and lesbian people are as such not any less mentally healthy than their straight friends there is no justification for subjecting gay candidates to more vigorous testing and scrutiny. Gay and straight candidates face the same essential difficulties.

How can they transfer the close friends and relationships from outside the community to inside the community? How can they learn to relate to all community members — regardless of ages, jobs, and personalities? How can they learn to relate to members of both the same and opposite sex? How can they learn to minister to God's people? How can they grow into a deep and loving relationship with God? (Marguerite Kropinak, 'Homosexuality and Religious Life' in Robert Nugent, *A Challenge to Love*, p. 254)

Some dioceses and religious congregations outside Britain have introduced mandatory HIV testing on all candidates. Again many have regarded this as a prejudiced attempt to flush out gay candidates. If this is the case then again the institution needs to acknowledge this. If the HIV test is simply part of a rigorous medical then candidates must know what a positive result would mean — would it mean instant rejection, in a way that having cancer or other serious diseases no longer automatically entails? There is something morally dubious about forcing a man to take a test which, whether positive or negative, will have repercussions on his financial status at the very least. Those responsible for screening candidates need to ask themselves whether prejudice should be good enough reason to override a divine call.

Seminaries and religious congregations have long had to deal with students falling in love with one another and engaging in sexual activity. For many years 'particular friendships' between students were taboo and stamped upon immediately but in more recent times friendships between students have come to be regarded as good and part of their formation in relationships. Brian was one of several priests who found the secrecy surrounding relationships at seminary painful. Such secrecy can encourage manipulation and abuse of the vulnerable. Some institutions automatically expel students found to be engaging in sexual relationships but since celibacy is now recognized to be a process to be learnt rather than an automatic gift some institutions are beginning to acknowledge that there will always be mistakes and lapses which can be turned into positive learning experiences.

The person may realize his/her human weakness — as well as his/her total dependence on and need for God — in order to fulfil the vow of celibacy. Reflection of the feelings and experience can lead to a renewed decision and commitment to celibacy as a response to God's love – a love now experienced, and known in a profound and personal way.

Finally the experience of falling in love can lead to the experience of being in love. Being in love is the growth experience which continues to occur when the intense feelings and the amount of time spent together lessens. This experience can lead to a deepening in prayer life and in the relationship with God. Love takes on the experience of knowing hurt from another; of sharing suffering with another; of experiencing both closeness and distance, as well as togetherness and separation; of knowing deepened joy and deepened appreciation; of knowing boredom with another and a willingness to just be with another. All these experiences can lead to a deepening revelation of the God who is love. (Marguerite Kropinak, 'Homosexuality and Religious Life' in Robert Nugent, *A Challenge to Love*, pp. 252–3)

For this positive reflection to happen seminaries have to face up to the reality of gay students within their doors and provide the right atmosphere and space for such reflection. Support groups for gay candidates are a necessary starting-point for such reflection. These, however, would have to be set up and run with sensitivity to prevent polarizing gay and straight students. Staff and all the students need to be properly educated in the latest scientific and theological understandings of homosexuality. Equality in treatment of persistently sexually active candidates must be ensured, though gay behaviour will be more obvious in a single-sex atmosphere. Once again an openness about this issue will ensure that seminarians can seriously consider whether celibacy is a viable way of life for them. The goal must always be maturity rather than blind obedience. Openly gay staff can provide a vital witness to the possibility of being a gay priest.

The institutions also need to be aware that they may receive adverse publicity if they accept openly gay candidates and they need to decide in advance how they will react to such exposure. Such honesty and commitment to facing reality will benefit all candidates.

An effective process provides an atmosphere of openness and trust about human sexuality, intimacy, and relationships which empowers individuals to discern freely the actions of God's grace as it mixes with their unique personalities and sexual journeys. This kind of ongoing process is both demanding and arduous, but there is no simple replacement to insure that candidates are given the professional, spiritual, and pastoral helps that will most effectively bring higher calibre ministers into the service of the church. (Robert Nugent, 'Seminary and Religious Candidates' in Robert Nugent and Jeannine Gramick, *Building Bridges*, p. 110)

As Will notes, 'If you are going to have a crisis with sexuality then it would be better to have it in the caring community that a seminary should be than out in a parish.' A great deal of work needs to be done to make seminaries caring communities for gay men and as Thomas notes 'there are lots of us about'.

'Ill-informed, lacking in understanding and compassion'

Attitudes to the Church's teaching on homosexuality

Gay priests are in an unenviable position with regards to the Congregation for the Doctrine of Faith's teaching on homosexuality. As gay people they are declared to be objectively disordered and a danger to society by the Church they serve and as priests they are expected to give pastoral care to lesbian and gay people in accordance with the teaching set out in the 1986 letter. As one priest put it:

> The 1986 letter only confirmed what I suspected — to be gay is not to be accepted by the Church and I am a priest of that Church. I am a split personality. I was hurt by the 1986 letter but heartened by the English bishops' statement and the American bishops' 1990 statement.

The questionnaire asked for views on the Church's teaching and reaction to the 1986 letter (the questionnaire was sent out before the 1992 letter had been published). Readers were specifically asked if the 1986 letter had changed their behaviour or attitudes in any way. Of the priests and seminarians who took part in the survey two had not read the 1986 letter and one had not even heard of it. However, all were aware of the basic Vatican teaching on homosexuality. Two priests felt that there were aspects of the 1986 letter to be welcomed, particularly its recognition that homosexual people need pastoral care and its recognition that the homosexual condition was not a sin in itself (although this was in fact qualified in the letter). The majority of the priests, however, simply believe the teaching articulated in the 1986 letter to be wrong.

> I don't accept the Church's teaching or to be more accurate the

teaching of the magisterium. There are many individuals within the Church who teach a much more positive approach to homosexuality which for me forms part of the Church's teaching. The magisterium for me just doesn't know what it is talking about, it speaks from a position of ignorance and bigotry and as a result my conscience tells me to ignore it. For me God has created me as a gay person. God does not create evil and he has given me a gift to be shared and used. I therefore not only condone gay relationships but encourage them as an essential way of using the gift God has given. The letter of 1986 initially made me very angry but I came to see it as it really is, 'not worth the paper it is written on'. There is no arguing about it: Ratzinger is wrong and therefore I disregard what he has to say. It still makes me angry when I think of the pain and suffering that letter has caused to many people and of the way it is used by conservative elements in the Church to justify their stand on homosexuality. It did not change my behaviour one bit except to make me more militant than ever.

This distinction between the teaching of the magisterium and the rest of the Church is one made by several of the priests. These men hold on to the teaching of Vatican II which emphasized that the whole people of God has a role in formulating Church teaching and that papal pronouncements require the assent of the Church, the *sensus fidelium*, to be an authentic definition of the issue.

With the help of the Holy Spirit, it is the task of the whole people of God, particularly of its pastors and theologians, to listen to and distinguish the many voices of our times and to interpret them in the light of the divine Word, in order that the revealed truth may be more deeply penetrated, better understood, and more suitably presented ... the faithful, both clerical and lay, should be accorded a lawful freedom of inquiry, of thought, and of expression. (*Gaudium et Spes: Pastoral Constitution on the Church in the Modern World*, 44 and 62)

Or, as the theologian Bernard Haering put it, a statement 'is not true merely because authority says so; rather it can be asserted and taught authoritatively only to the extent that it can be proven true' (Sipe, *A Secret World*, p. 28). It can be argued that the Vatican's pronouncements on homosexuality are not 'the Church's teaching', but are simply statements from the magisterium, to be taken seriously though not as a criterion for loyalty to the Church. The Church's teaching is not yet properly formulated, study of the subject still goes on in all parts of the world in the light of scientific, biological and psychological discoveries and philosophical debate. It appears that many gay priests cope with the Vatican teaching by holding on to this wide definition of the Church.

On the business of 'disloyalty to the Church', for a long time and in a mild sort of way, I have mentally separated the Church as organism, Body of Christ, Temple of the Spirit, and its other august and deep titles from the more human elements which extend from 'Father's too long/badly prepared sermon' to what sometimes issues from Rome. When it is necessary to separate the two in one's own mind, and to plump for what one believes is Christ's Church, I have had no difficulty in living with this.

The problem is that, as noted in the introduction, the Vatican seems to have jettisoned this model of the Church and assumed all authority to itself, returning to a distinction between the *ecclesia docens* (the teaching Church) — the Vatican — and the *ecclesia discens* (the learning Church) — the rest of the Church.

Several priests also noted that they found the attitude to homosexuality in the 1986 letter irreconcilable with their personal experience of life as a gay man.

I must say that I find the Church's teaching on homosexuality difficult to come to terms with. Although I can understand how the present teaching developed I cannot square it with my own experience of being a homosexual. On one level I keep separate my understanding of the Church's teaching and my own conviction and feeling that my gayness is something good and that gay relationships can be very good and I am sure very acceptable to the Lord. On a deeper level, maybe I am happy to be Catholic and to be gay. In myself I seem to be able to bring the two dimensions together. I seem to remember that when the 'Halloween' letter came out in 1986 I felt taken aback and to a degree angry. The letter did not really change my attitudes. It seemed to confirm me in my determination to be Catholic and gay. Also it strengthened my conviction that the Church has got the question of homosexuality wrong.

I think the Church's teaching on homosexuality is ill-informed, lacking in compassion and understanding of human nature, and very little to do with what I understand my relationship to be with Christ. I know that he loves me as I am, which is more than can be said for the Church. My reaction to the 1986 letter on the pastoral care of homosexual persons was fatalistic. Nothing seemed to have changed, I am still considered to be an 'intrinsically disordered person'.

It did not change my behaviour or attitudes in any way whatsoever. Frankly I found it had nothing to say to me in the reality in which I find myself. In other words it was irrelevant to my life.

Two priests noted that it was painfully obvious that the Vatican had not consulted 'those who have personal experience of the topics upon which they pontificate'.

I have come to believe that because one's sexual orientation is so basic to a person, that really it is only gays who can understand gayness. Heterosexual people can only see something abstract, something right outside of themselves, something they believe they can understand but which they can never appreciate; and so because the Church's teachers are heterosexual or purporting thus to be, the heterosexual perspective should be expected to show through.

One priest said that what upset him most was the 'people who came to confession feeling more ostracized than ever' after reading or hearing about the 1986 letter. Like Simon most priests detected a growing understanding and acceptance of homosexuals in the *sensus fidelium*. David, along with an increasing number of Vatican watchers, sees parallels between the Vatican and the old rulers of Eastern Europe who refused to face up to reality, listen to their people and ruled through dictatorial power, crushing dissent. David believes that the Vatican will soon have to deal with a revolution led by the laity on issues like homosexuality and he warns 'gay men have long memories and will remember those who came to their assistance and those who were first to cast stones'. He would no doubt believe that the 1992 letter with its instruction to American bishops to oppose anti-discrimination legislation has brought that revolution closer.

None of the priests changed their fundamental behaviour or attitudes as a result of the 1986 letter, although it did make two

more radical in their approach to lesbian and gay issues, one more
angry with the Church, and one became more discreet.

Twelve of the priests and seminarians thought that the magisterium should approach the subject of homosexuality as a justice issue
as well as a matter of morality, that is to say that the Church should
be concerned with the human and civil rights of homosexual
persons. They therefore find themselves once again in disagreement
with the Vatican.

> For me the Church needs to get away from the moral issues and
> start looking at the areas of justice concerning gay people. I think
> the Church hides behind the moral stance as an excuse not to face
> up to the justice issues involved. Even if you are a traditional and
> very conservative member of the Church and accept the Church's
> teaching on homosexuality, the Church's teaching on human
> rights and the dignity of the human person would demand that
> you act to defend the rights of gay people. In addition gay people
> are members of the Church and they have the same rights as their
> heterosexual counterparts. It is for me much more an issue of
> justice than morality.

> The Church needs to be more pastoral and less dogmatic. The
> Church should speak out more in justice and peace issues. It would
> be better being silent on morals!

> Homosexuality is both a moral and a justice issue. The Church
> must realize that moral goal-posts move from one generation to
> the next and are not static. Only when the Church sees the
> homosexual life-style as morally acceptable will its persecution of
> lesbians and gay men cease. I believe in positive action, theological
> and practical, to bring about this change.

Three priests admitted that they were not brave enough to take up
the cause of lesbian and gay people in terms of justice.

Most of the priests and seminarians surveyed have managed to find a
way of dealing with the Vatican statements on homosexuality that
protects their integrity as gay men. The teaching enshrined in the
documents of the Second Vatican Council have helped to distinguish
between the teaching of the magisterium and the Church as a whole.
Vatican II also emphasized the value of experience in developing
teaching. For most of the men surveyed there was a dissonance

between the understanding of homosexuality that lay behind the Vatican letter and their experience as gay men. One gets the impression that they have grown in their understanding of sexuality while the Church has trodden water. There is no evidence at all that the priests believed the Vatican statements to be conveying the will of God. One priest summarized his views succinctly:

> We are not school-children, whether we are Catholics or whoever we are. We are meant to be mature. It is not just that the Pope says, or the bishops say, or the priest says and we click our heels and obey. You have to be true to the God you know.

Glad to be gay?

The priests and seminarians were asked in the questionnaire whether they were glad to be gay. This was to ascertain how many were 'ego-dystonic' with regards to their sexuality, that is unable to accept it as good and unable to integrate it into the rest of their persons and lives. The answers given fall into three broad categories: 'Yes', 'Yes, but' and 'No'. Ten of the respondents simply answered the question 'yes', some adding 'very' or 'definitely', one admitting 'that it doesn't figure much in my life — one just gets on with daily living, gay or otherwise'. Those who answered 'Yes' tended to be those who knew they were gay before they entered seminary and had come to accept themselves as such at quite an early age. Nine of the respondents answered 'Yes, but'. These tended to be men like Brian, David and Simon who had come to acceptance to their sexuality only after a very long and painful struggle.

> I believe that in the eyes of God gayness is morally indifferent and insofar as all people share his love so do gays. So I am spiritually very happy being gay. However, on the other side, I accept it as a limiting condition on my life (requiring concealment, patience when hearing what some people in the context of the Church say about it, and so on); but I also believe that most people have to live with limiting conditions (from public loyalty to married partner, to keeping one's own weaknesses or emotions out of sight of other people, and so on).

> The short answer to this question is yes! But it hasn't always been the case. I can remember the times I used to sit and pray, asking God to make me straight like everyone else and I can even

remember the bargains I used to make with God. I can remember the times as a student for the priesthood when I would be scared to death that someone would find out and that it would end my hopes of life in the ministry. Gradually I came to accept my sexuality as a gift from God, a gift to be enjoyed, celebrated and used. I can honestly say that now I wouldn't want to be any different, I can actually thank God for creating me a gay person.

Yes I am, but I have only reached that point after a long and tortuous journey. I think I finally came to terms with my sexuality about seven years ago; as I am now 49, it was a long time. Up until I was 42 I had very serious doubts about my value as a person and as a priest, and deep concern as to how my spiritual well-being was affected by my orientation. Did God really love me as I was? In the end an elderly lady friend told me 'he made you the way you are, and he loves his creation'. I think that was the beginning of coming to terms with myself.

I'm as happy to be gay as I'll ever be. I'm fairly happy these days but I can't say this happiness was easily arrived at. I never thought too highly of the gay human condition as I grew up. I placed a high value on the heterosexual condition and perceived as I still do perceive that marriage and family life following from the heterosexual condition are things I've been done out of in virtue of my being gay. Curiously enough, some years ago my brother asked me if I'd become a priest just because I was gay. I answered 'No, but had I not been gay I greatly doubt I should have become a priest'. I think I would have opted for marriage and family life. So I've come to terms with it, I've never been happy about it but at least I can live with it. As to recruiting one more priest to the clergy's ranks it may be a question of 'God works in mysterious ways'.

These 'Yes, but' men tended to be people who had some knowledge of their sexuality before going into the seminary but were deeply disturbed by their orientation and remained so for many years. Some like Mark spent many years trying to sublimate their desires and emotional needs, hoping that they would just 'go away', believing that God could not love them as gay men. A few of these priests, like David and Simon, only began to accept their sexuality after some sort of crisis connected with their sexuality which forced them to face themselves honestly. For one priest this crisis was set within the context of an exorcism conducted by fellow members of the charismatic renewal movement. The priest now believes that part of the reason he was attracted to this movement was that it gave him a 'safe' context in which to express his sexuality through hugs, kisses, talk of love, etc.

> There were a lot of people who found it safe to touch, to hug and to kiss as celibate sisters and priests in a prayer group context. In any other context they would be very worried but they knew they could touch. They felt safe because it was purely within a religious, spiritual context. Any suggestion of homosexuality and you would be prayed over for deliverance or something of that sort. I was. I was persuaded that I wanted it. Anything but a heterosexual outlook was anti-biblical in their eyes. I know of situations now of people who have come to me for help after being prayed over and I see now where I was at. You get prayed over and then you feel very free [of homosexuality] and then, a little while later, you are not feeling free at all. Something else comes up. You start to realize that there is another dimension to your life that is sexual so a touch or a kiss or a hug has that aspect to it. Then you feel guilty and impure. They were trying to deliver me from spirit possession — 'the spirit of lust', 'the spirit of homosexuality' would be the ones they describe and they would pray over you intensely, calling out the spirit.

Two respondents declared themselves not happy to be gay. Seminarian Will, although now 'at home' with his sexuality in that he is no longer fighting against it, believes that no one can be happy being part of a minority which is treated so badly by society at large and by the Catholic Church in particular. He would also have liked to have had a family. Two other well-integrated priests also admit to mourning the possibility of having children. The other priest regrets his gayness for reasons similar to Will's:

> No. I would like to be but years of 'being different' and not being accepted by society, family, church and friends makes me feel alienated from others and induces me to shyness — a 'loner' and being very hurt in the very depths of my being.

Mark envies those priests who have managed to integrate their sexuality into their lives and priesthood.

Priests and seminarians were asked to share positive or negative experiences in the Church as a result of their sexuality. Two priests could not provide any instances because they are not 'out' in any manner at all.

> On reflection, I think the answer is no. This is mainly because I have not found it difficult (temperamentally, again) to live a life of concealment, and this includes an ability to turn off when silly things are said, regardless of how senior or influential the speaker might be.

> No, because I have kept things to myself mainly but have to pick up the pieces sometimes, helping some who have been rejected and refused the sacraments because of their 'orientation'.

Brian and Simon had both been through the much-feared experience of being 'outed', Simon very publicly. Whilst both of these men acknowledge that these were horrendous experiences at the time, they have come to regard them as having positive value in that they felt freed from fear of being exposed and feel that they now live their lives with more integrity as out gay men. David had had to leave active ministry for a year having fallen in love with someone but had returned stronger and more integrated as a gay man and priest and has since found himself able to identify with other oppressed groups and has found a strength to speak out against injustice.

Most other priests listed both positive and negative experiences. Among the negative were these:

> The only negative attitude I have ever encountered has been through the official teaching of the Church. This has alienated me to the extent that I don't suppose I take very much notice of what the Church has to say.

> A couple of attempts at blackmail when the bishop (not the present one) was very supportive though not coming out in the open about his own attitudes on the subject.

> The older generation, I think, don't expect us to be sexual at all.

> A priest friend suggested that we should break off contact as a result of my telling him in confession. I am tired of being the butt of horrid jokes and having to say nothing or turning the conversation.

I had one difficult experience when I was in a parish where there was a young person who was very upset about his own sexuality, he was involved in the gay scene as well as the Church and he knew of my gay contacts. I was a source of confusion to him so I got moved from that parish. From a very busy parish to a remote corner of the diocese with a parish priest who I felt was homophobic and probably gay too. I think the young person had sought advice from other priests who had compounded his guilt and he reported to them what I had said to him. They felt — he and I were friends — that we were dealing in an area that was very dangerous, that it would be better for me not to be involved there because I would be saying the wrong things in terms of what the Church taught. Instead of talking about it, the Church wanted to palm it off, and palm me off to counselling.

Of the seminarians, Thomas found diocesan selection psychological tests profoundly 'disturbing, unfair and hurtful', presumably because he felt they were in part designed to expose gay men. Vernon wrote of the 'implicit rejection' by other students and Will had the not uncommon experience of being refused absolution and castigated by a priest in confession.

But there were also plenty of positive experiences. Most of them were unostentatious experiences of acceptance from other people.

I have met many good loving people who by their Christian life have shown me that it is possible to be gay, to be a gay priest, to have a partner, and still have a fruitful and enjoyable ministry as a priest. In the end those are the people one takes notice of, not some Vatican bureaucrat stuck in an office divorced from reality and life.

I think my own sexuality has made me more able to help others with problems of all sorts and my own weakness has made me more compassionate to others.

The love, support and friendship of those who know me and my past but still love me.

Those who know of my sexuality especially in the parish here are very supportive and accept me as a whole person who serves them as a priest. I have never had a really negative reaction from anyone I have come out to but there again I choose those people very carefully. In particular the youth group here (17 +) are very accepting and supportive.

I've never had any rejection. I've had a lot of understanding and compassion from those of the clergy who are not gay who I have spoken to about this although they are not very many.

Those who know I'm gay are grateful for my coming out to them because it has helped them to be more open about their sexuality and problems associated with integrating it in their lives.

I suppose I would belong to those who would say that being a priest is a good way to channel your gay sexuality.

Of being sexually vulnerable — yes it helps in the Sacrament of Reconciliation hetero/homo. Helping other gay people feel okay about themselves and God.

Such examples of acceptance and affirmation are extremely important to gay priests who, much more than straight priests, fear and experience rejection by those with whom and for whom they work.

The overwhelming majority of the respondents to the questionnaire are happy to be gay. Many have gone through protracted periods of self-hatred and exhibited all the characteristics of an ego-dystonic personality but have emerged from that suffering as integrated, self-accepting, ego-syntonic gay men. Those that have emerged from what Simon describes as a self-imposed grave have usually managed to do so because of the affirmation and acceptance that they have received from people to whom they have 'come out'. In his survey of gay Catholic clergy in the United States James Wolf found that there, too, the majority of respondents 'self-identify as gay and accept that orientation as an important and productive component of their personalities' (*Gay Priests*, p. 73). The irony of all this is that these gay priests live up to Pope John Paul's vision of well-integrated, self-aware, sexually mature men in the priesthood. But in some quarters of the Church, at least, these men are not welcome in the priesthood because of their mental health. The American psychiatrist M. Scott Peck describes mental health as 'an ongoing process of dedication to reality at all costs'.

[The] tendency to avoid problems and the emotional suffering inherent in them is the primary basis of all human mental illness. ... Some of us will go to quite extraordinary lengths to avoid our problems and the suffering they cause, proceeding far afield from all that is clearly good and sensible in order to try to find an easy way out, building the most elaborate fantasies in which to live, sometimes to the total exclusion of reality. In the succinctly elegant words of Carl Jung, 'Neurosis is always a substitute for legitimate suffering'. (M. Scott Peck, *The Road Less Travelled: A New Psychology of Love, Traditional Values, and Spiritual Growth* [Arrow, London, 1990], pp. 14–15)

The Vatican seems to be committed to keeping its gay priests mentally ill: by denying their existence, dismissing their sexuality as disordered and dangerous and giving them no encouragement or opportunity to face the reality of their sexuality and work through it, an atmosphere is created in which such exploration is unacceptable. Some people in authority in the Church believe it is only those who cannot accept the reality of their homosexuality who should be admitted to the priesthood. Of course, as Scott Peck points out, we all have a tendency to try and avoid problems and parts of reality and so none of us is completely mentally well. But a person's sexuality is so central to them that to deny it or to try and avoid it is extremely dangerous. Sexuality is about love and relationships and, as Pope John Paul pointed out, it is through his capacity to relate to others and love that a priest primarily fulfils his ministry. When a priest or religious suffers from a neurotic attitude to his sexuality, when he is forced to live in 'the closet' unable to be open and content with his sexuality, his ministry will be disordered because he will be. At present the Vatican seems content to let a significant number of its priests suffer from mental ill-health which will undoubtedly restrict and damage their ministry. This is because in a sense the Vatican itself has a neurotic attitude to homosexuality in general and gay clergy in particular. It denies the realities of their ministry and simply concentrates on impractical plans to weed them out. It is quite extraordinary that so many priests and religious who are immersed in the life of the Church should have achieved self-acceptance and had the strength to battle against the forces in the Church that conspire to prevent such acceptance. That they have done so is a tribute to their inner strength, many years of struggle and also to the men and women who offer them unconditional love and acceptance. Mark envies his brother priests who have accepted themselves but, in the eyes of some, his suffering, pain, confusion and despair make him the better, more acceptable, gay priest.

Celibacy and sexual activity

The questionnaire asked whether the respondents were comfortable with the discipline of celibacy. They were also asked if they were sexually active and if so whether they felt guilty about this. In his survey of gay Catholic priests in the USA James Wolf found that out of 101 priests who replied to his questionnaire only one had not engaged in any sexual activity since ordination. In Wolf's survey 63 per cent of gay priests found leading a celibate life a frequent source of problems, compared with 11 per cent of priests in general. 58.6 per cent of the gay priests in his survey felt that celibacy was an ideal to be worked towards rather than a law to be obeyed. 35.4 per cent understood celibacy simply as the commitment not to marry rather than as a commitment to abstain from all sexual activity. 33.3 per cent were still uncertain about what celibacy actually meant. 41.4 per cent considered their sexual life as separate from their life as a priest (*Gay Priests*, pp. 26, 36–8). In terms of attitudes to celibacy and sexual activity the British gay priests surveyed share some but, significantly, not all of the attitudes and experiences of their brothers in the USA. Not one of the British respondents described themselves as being comfortable with the discipline of celibacy. Most, like Simon, thought that compulsory celibacy for the clergy was unnecessary and in many cases destructive.

Over the years of seminary training I accepted the discipline of celibacy—at least in my conscious self. There was probably the feeling that accepting ordination and celibacy was an honourable way of coping with one's sexuality. At the present time I am ambivalent towards celibacy. On balance, looking at the Church's history, I think that mandatory celibacy has done more harm than good.

I think celibacy will go after the present pontificate.

I am not comfortable with the discipline of celibacy. For me the ideal situation would be for me to be able to be openly in a committed relationship and continue to minister as a priest in much the same way that I think heterosexual priests should be free to marry.

I believe this discipline is quite wrong and that it should be abolished as an obligation for the Western Church. Priests should be free to choose celibacy permanently or temporarily just like any other members of the Church. I have belonged to the Movement for the Ordination of Married Men from its inception.

I become more dubious about the value of sexual abstinence for most people today, though many would want to make sexual intimacy optional rather than compulsory. For many, if not most, such expression could help rather than hinder their ministry by making them a more fulfilled and contented person.

I do not think that the Church has thought through what celibacy means. It was easier before the Second Vatican Council when mass was celebrated with the priest with his back to the people. He had no contact with them. But now when he says 'The Lord be with you', he expects them to reply, looking at him. And his body language — how he speaks, how he holds himself, all of that communicates his in-touch-ness with who he is. And of course for many priests they were never called to celibacy, they were called to priesthood but they have taken on celibacy as a second thing that goes with it. They have never had a charism to celibacy. So they are uncomfortable with it and they do not like people getting close to them. Priests who will only let people into the waiting room, that kind of attitude, they always wear black, keeping people at a distance, as protection. All of that is because they are not in touch with who they are. They keep the drawbridge up so they are safe and maybe they need some drink to keep them going but they keep people at a certain distance from them so that they don't invade the priests' space and make them worry about their celibacy. If a priest is really a celibate he can kiss and hug and feel fine and if more priests did that it would be much healthier.

A number of priests and one of the seminarians noted that they felt called to priesthood but not to celibacy; celibacy came along with the job and so they attempted to take it on board. As one priest noted:

> When you are preparing for the priesthood, your goal is ordination, your spiritual sights are very high, your generosity to God is bordering on the heroic, and you accept the discipline of celibacy in that context. While some life-long decisions have to be made, the one concerning celibacy is difficult to defend conclusively or to shoot down equally conclusively.

None of the three seminarian respondents, however, made any attempt to defend the discipline of celibacy: two admitted that they could find no justification for it and one acknowledged that it was going to be a struggle. Two of the seminarians took the requirement very seriously and aspired to the ideal. Vernon, however, disclosed that he would not avoid a relationship if it 'turned up'.

Will noted that celibacy was not something he could do on his own and Thomas made the point that being a celibate is not to be a bachelor but to be a lover — that is to say, to be celibate is to be in relationship with others, 'the love of many' as he puts it. But, as Simon points out, the priests' experience is often not of love from parish or from the wider Church but of loneliness, isolation, a sense of unappreciation and constant change which prevents the formation of deep relationships. This can be intensified for gay priests by the isolation and fear that comes from feeling the need to hide part of one's nature. Mark makes the point that he needs love 'personally' and finds the level of love offered to him as a priest too shallow and impersonal. Two other priests noted that it was not sexual activity or the lack of it that caused them most pain but the lack of intimate relationships with other people, relationships in which one is valued, affirmed and empowered.

> Genital activity was never really what I wanted but 'connectedness' of spirit, intimacy, etc.

Unlike their American counterparts these British priests made no attempt to define celibacy only in terms of a commitment not to marry. They understand it, as the Church authorities and their congregations do, in terms of complete abstinence from sexual relationships. But like the American priests most of the respondents admitted to sexual activity since ordination. Some indicated that they had been sexually active before beginning their training. Brian had his first sexual experience with an older priest. Nine men are currently sexually active and they have varying degrees of guilt.

On sexual activity I have taken the line that I don't feel it is wrong, but that it is very wrong if it is allowed to give scandal (the priesthood is a public office). So, whatever some might think about demeaning oneself, I feel it is responsible always to go far away and into another diocese.

I have been sexually active. I do feel guilty but I do not think I should have been made to do something I find at violence with myself.

Yes there are times when I am sexually active and guilt is not a feeling I experience very often. If anything it has a positive effect on my priestly ministry, it certainly has a positive effect on my life as a human being. The only negative aspect is the fear of disclosure — not because of myself but because I would then be expected to make a choice between ministry and sexual activity. This has become especially difficult when I have fallen in love with someone and formed a close relationship. Eventually a decision has to be made, relationship or ministry. Up to now ministry has always come first.

I think that you would need to make the distinction between normally active and the very occasional lapse. Certainly I feel that a sexually active priesthood is not compatible. Celibacy, however, is something to be worked at, like a marriage. It doesn't simply happen which I suspect is how many view it. As someone once said to me, there are no scissors! Much of the time not a problem. Possibly because of good friends. Relationships are very important to me — with both sexes. Lack of sexual activity is usually not the problem. Loneliness, isolation, certainly is.

Only four priests feel guilty about sexual activity and five state that they believe that sexual activity has actually enhanced their ministry and made them better priests. Three, who are living in long-term partnerships with other men, believe that this relationship enriches their lives and ministry.

I have been sexually active for most of my ministry, at first with a great sense of guilt because these were not open and accepted relationships but latterly I have come to accept my relationship as being one of the most important factors in making me the sort of priest that I am and I have been blessed with being in my present relationship for some twelve years.

I am sexually active, and have had a very intimate relationship with another man for the last 7 years. This has not inhibited my ministry as a priest, in fact I believe, in fact I know, that it has enriched my ministry and has given me a greater sensitivity in dealing with other people. I must say that I do not feel guilty about this. Should you feel guilt because you love another person who loves you, and which enables you to do what is required of you?

I still feel guilty about [the discipline of celibacy], but less and less. I do have a relationship which I have had for about sixteen years, and would be devastated without such a close companion. The affect it has on my ministry is one of compassion and understanding, in all forms of counselling, with gays or others.

These priests stand in sharp contrast to some of their colleagues in the USA who draw a psychological line between their priesthood and sexual activity. Mark was not the only priest to dream of being able to set up house with another man.

Only four priests, including Brian, described themselves as celibate, although Brian has had to resist advances from older priests. Three felt it made their ministry easier because there would be some conflict between the demands of a relationship and those of a priestly life.

I find for myself that I'm not the sort of person to get very far with over-intense relationships and they start to use up energy. I enjoy my life and I get involved with people. When I'm involved with a gay group it is because I believe in it, it is not because I'm looking for a relationship. Looking back over the years at the few individuals who have come out for me as special I've felt very destabilized by them. I am not very good at handling a close one to one. I need a bit of freedom, a bit of space, at the same time as having folk around me. [Being celibate] makes life less complicated, saves risk and danger. A gay lodger gives me companionship and physical affection. That is enough.

I used to be sexually active but never felt good about it — mixture of guilt and deceit of living a double life ... My God is incarnate in the person of Jesus with whom I've had an intimate relationship since childhood. He helps me remain celibate.

Two of the celibate priests noted that they did engage in masturbation, one, Brian, finding it to be a source of guilt.

A couple of gay men in our survey are living celibate lives, some live celibate lives for most of the time, but occasionally lapse, and some no longer regard celibacy as an ideal to be striven for but can only find fulfilment in sexual relationships, some long-term. Many doubt the validity of compulsory celibacy for the secular priesthood whilst some acknowledge that it is a necessary discipline for religious brothers living in a community where the coupling up of community members, or relationships with men outside the community, could have a negative impact on the life of the community. Of course the experiences and attitudes of these gay men only reflects the wider celibacy crisis in the Church. They share with thousands of their heterosexual colleagues the pain of sometimes having to choose between a vocation to the priesthood and love of another person, the pain of guilt and loneliness, and the pain of secrecy. But in some ways the plight of gay clergy on this issue is worse than that for other priests. For a start, it is very unlikely that gay clergy will have received any education for celibacy as *gay* men, with attention paid to their particular situation. Sipe notes that celibacy can only be achieved through self-knowledge, a proper understanding of the process of celibacy and examples to follow.

Since celibacy is the redirection of sexual energy from its original goal of direct discharge to both delayed and derivative gratification, it cannot be attained by a simple act of will. (*A Secret World*, p. 237)

Gay clergy are not receiving proper education for celibacy. And whereas there is empathy and understanding in some parts of the Church, at least, for heterosexual clergy who find celibacy impossible, there is practically none for gay clergy in Britain who do not have the support groups, counselling organizations or recognition of their plight granted to their heterosexual brothers. Homosexual relationships are regarded by society in general as unnatural, nasty and dangerous and by the Church as sinful. This adds to the strain on the gay priest under the discipline of celibacy. There is no safe haven in the Church or in the world. But for some priests it is this lack of a safe haven within the institution they serve that propels them into relationships with other gay men. Their partners give them the support and affirmation and personal love they need to be good priests, in a way that the Church refuses, and often at great personal cost to themselves, having to keep their relationship secret and unacknowledged for the sake of the priest. It is interesting that only Mark notes the problems faced by partners of gay priests. The voice of women involved with priests is only just beginning to be heard. Gay partners will share some of the suffering of these women — isolation, insecurity, guilt, the strain of having to keep relationships secret, being blamed for leading the priest astray, knowing that sometimes if it came to a choice between a relationship or priesthood they would be discarded. Once again secrecy obliterates responsibility and the Church's record in dealing with priests' lovers is not good.

If the Church wants its priests to remain celibate then it must provide a proper formation in this area to seminarians, but also to ordained priests, and it must ensure that a priest's emotional needs are catered for in terms of support and companionship, particularly at times of crisis. This will mean recognizing the particular needs and problems facing gay men. But the time has come to face the reality that there are gay priests and that some of them are sexually active, some in long-term relationships. Their testimony must be taken into account with all the other evidence that celibacy is not an achievable or sometimes desirable goal for many men called to the priesthood. What becomes clear from reading the responses to the questionnaire is that the gay priests who are sexually active are not depraved, irresponsible men who have little regard for their priesthood. They are dedicated priests who have usually been through huge crises of conscience and much pain in arriving at their present status, celibate or non-celibate. They all need love.

Seeking support

In *Pastores Dabo Vobis* Pope John Paul II recognized the need for suitable support structures for all priests and he encouraged all members of the Church to support their pastors. Loneliness and isolation are common problems among all priests but seem to be particularly problematic for gay priests. In his survey Wolf found that whereas only 14.8 per cent of all clergy found the loneliness of the priesthood a frequent problem, 44 per cent of gay clergy found it a frequent problem (*Gay Priests*, p. 26). This is a sad and serious situation for, as Tony Philpot has written,

> [Priests] wither if we have no one to confide in, no one to offer us unconditional support, no one who knows us as we really are and *still accepts us*. Too often there is the feeling of living a lie, of bluffing the public, including our colleagues. 'If they knew what I was really like, they'd want no more to do with me.' ... I think this is the greatest sacrifice involved in celibacy. (Tony Philpot, *Brothers in Christ: A Call to Fraternity in the Diocesan Priesthood* [Kevin Mayhew, Bury St Edmunds, 1991], pp. 57–8)

A gay priest may feel that he risks rejection because of his homosexuality if he were to reveal it or it became known to fellow priests, his spiritual director, bishop or superior, or even to lay friends. Some of those surveyed felt their sexuality seriously affected their relationships with other priests:

> I can never be myself with them unless they know and then talk often degenerates to sexual jokes. Among straight priests I can never be myself. I wish I could be.

Those [priests] who know fall into two categories — those who accept me, either because they are gay or because they accept me as a person and those who are not comfortable. Within my religious community there are a good number who know. Some are OK, others are two-faced, but I am not going to apologize for myself to anyone so they can take me or leave me. Then there are those who don't know. This group causes me the most problems either because I sometimes feel I am being dishonest and sometimes because of their attitude to gay people I feel real anger towards them.

I am not very happy in clerical company at the best of times and find my natural milieu amongst the ordinary people of God. I think I am quite anti-clerical and look forward to the end of the clerical caste as we have known it as the present clergy die off and are not replaced.

Sometimes they [other priests] have their own problems which are challenged by my own comfortableness in the area of sexuality.

One man discussed his sexuality with a fellow priest during confession. After that the priest refused to speak to him. Simon finds himself in 'voluntary exile' and unsure of the affection and support of his diocesan colleagues since his sexuality became public knowledge. Only one priest found that his sexuality did not affect his relationship with other clergy. Those priests who know other gay priests found the friendship of these men very helpful and supportive. But, as David notes, it is ironic that there appear to be so many gay clergy and yet so few support networks for them.

The networks that I find helpful are those that accept me as a person who also happens to be a priest rather than those who see me as a priest first. The network of friends that I have built up with other gay priests is very precious to me as are the friendships I have formed with gay people who are not priests but who accept me as a human being first.

Five priests mentioned that they belonged to gay organizations. Four of those belonged to Quest or LGCM and all found them helpful, although one priest noted:

Quest is fine but I find when I do meet a group from there, which is very infrequently, one is needed for counselling or confession and one is considered to be a bit strange, or they do not want to know if the clergy need to talk.

A couple of priests mentioned a small informal network of gay priests across the country which produces a newsletter. However, much as this was appreciated by the priests involved they thought the ideal would be to have local networks. Although there is always the problem that most gay clergy would fear becoming involved in an openly gay organization, particularly within their own diocese.

One priest regretted that diocesan Ministry to Priests groups, which exist to support diocesan clergy, did not deal with sexuality at all:

> But I remember a while back when we had a study day for chaplains to Quest and other priests. And they said they were worried about how they'd let their parish priest or their curate know they were coming to such a day. They were frightened that anyone would look at their literature, go into their rooms, discover where they were going, or what the nuns in the convent might repeat to somebody else. They were showing paranoid attitudes. Once you get beyond that, you accept that there must be a risk involved. Then you can meet with other priests and talk about spirituality and sexuality. I think a lot could happen, although it may not be possible to organize something on diocesan level. Everyone would have to accept that the others may not be within the laws of the Church. If one priest was out 'on the scene', going to gay clubs, it would be no good at all if the others were horrified because he would never talk about that. It has got to be a safe place. At the moment there is so much fear among priests about sexuality that it will not happen.

Three priests regarded their spiritual directors as their main source of support. One priest who had been living with a partner for many years noted that his partner was his 'greatest support'. Two men found their primary support in local secular gay organizations. One mentioned his family and two mentioned professional counsellors. One priest found his parish youth group very supportive.

All clergy are under the authority of either a bishop or a religious superior. He is their 'boss' and determines where they work and for how long, but he is also their pastor, the person responsible for their emotional and physical well-being. This puts both bishops and clergy in an impossible position. In theory a priest suffering any difficulties in ministry should share those difficulties with his bishop who will take the appropriate pastoral action, but if a priest fears that sharing his sexuality with his bishop might get him into trouble, have him moved or forced into unwanted therapy (a common response), the relationship breaks down. The priest suffers alone, he dare not seek help or support, with potentially grave results for himself and the people to whom he is a pastor. Four of the men who took part in the survey knew that their bishop or superior was aware of their sexuality. All seemed to be happy with the situation although not without some misgivings:

> My superior knows that I am gay and to a certain extent I think I can count on his support although I am not sure he is being totally honest with me in that I have discovered that I am not considered for certain appointments — not because of my sexuality but because I am too open about it. Well, I'm not going back in the closet for anyone!

A common comment from those who had told their bishop or superior was that they were aware that they were very lucky in having supportive men as their pastors. Most were uncomfortable with the thought that the present bishop or superior might be replaced by a more conservative man, a practice which seems to have become a policy in the pontificate of John Paul II. Most of those who had not told their bishop or superior seemed convinced that he would be very unsupportive and that 'coming out' to such people was a dangerous act. None of the seminarians had told their bishop. One stated that he considered 'I would not be ordained' if the bishop knew.

We have already noted that Catholic lay people are not used to regarding their clergy as frail, vulnerable human beings with needs and problems. In an ideal Church the priest's first and most obvious means of support would lie with his people. However, one feels that in most parishes displays of honesty and vulnerability from priests would be likely to lead to complaints to the bishop and removal of the priest from the parish or other place of ministry. One priest in our survey had been hounded by a parishioner who simply suspected he might be gay. This one parishioner was making his life hell, complaining to the bishop, spreading rumour and misinformation around the parish and objecting to any changes or developments in the parish that the priest suggested or countenanced. In a homophobic society and homophobic Church, simply asking for help or support as a gay priest is a frightening and risky move.

In a pioneering study of homosexual clergy in the Church of England, Dr Ben Fletcher found that homosexual clergy showed disturbingly high levels of stress. He found that isolation, Church teaching on homosexuality, homophobia, the strain of having to pretend to be something one was not to parishioners, bishops and fellow clergy, combined with the stresses of a demanding vocation, all conspired to induce dangerously high levels of stress (Ben Fletcher, *Clergy Under Stress: A Study of Homosexual and Heterosexual Clergy* [Mowbray, London, 1990]). We have already noted that some Roman Catholic clergy who are gay share most of these concerns. Richard Sipe found that over 50 per cent of the homosexual clergy he surveyed had severe alcohol problems (*A Secret World*, p. 131). Dr Fletcher recommended that the Church of England recognize the need for 'the formation of an independent and confidential advisory and counselling service' which would be of benefit for all clergy. He also recommended that the Church allow and even encourage the setting up of nation-wide support groups for gay clergy. These are both ideas which the Catholic Church in this country would be advised to take up. But the authorities of both the Anglican and Catholic Churches steadfastly ignore the presence of large numbers of gay clergy in their midst, never mind the problems and stress factors that those men have to bear. Embarrassment triumphs over the Church's obligation to minister to its priests.

Those filling in the questionnaire were asked how much contact they had with the gay and lesbian community, that is to say, with secular lesbian and gay groups, gay pubs and clubs etc. Eight had no contact at all with the gay scene. Several of those who had no contact explained that this was because they were frightened of being 'outed', publicly exposed as gay. This fear is not without foundation. Two of the priests in the survey had been stalked by tabloid journalists. One priest also felt involvement with the gay community was incompatible with being a follower of Christ:

> The 'out' gay community can be threatening and dangerous and anti-Christian. I look for Christian (Catholic) principles.

Even those priests who do get involved in the gay scene exercise some discretion:

> Not in this area, it is too small a community and I fear blackmail.
> But I do try and join a 'community' celebration when I can away
> from here.

Priests not only risk exposure in the wider community by becoming
involved with the gay community. They also risk rejection from the
gay community, which is often rabidly anti-religious, if they 'come
out' as priests.

> I enjoy an evening out on the gay scene. I am out as a priest to
> some and not to others. I sometimes choose not to tell people that I
> am a priest because of the negative reactions you sometimes
> receive. For many people in gay organizations they tend to see you
> as the Roman Catholic Church incarnate and they relate to you in
> a negative way. For others they always seem to want to talk shop
> when you are out for a break from it all.

The questionnaire then asked priests whether they thought it
would be helpful to themselves or to other gay or lesbian Catholics if
there were more 'out' gay people in the local Church community.
Only one respondent answered with a resounding 'no'.

> Personally, no. I believe society is heterosexual and family-based.
> 'Out' gay people in the local Church community could, of course,
> be of great help and growth to each other; but how to organize
> such a thing without risking breaking up the community as well I
> don't know.

Other respondents expressed a strong desire that this could happen
whilst acknowledging the risks that would have to be taken and
making it clear that they did not approve of the practice of 'outing'.

> It would help a great deal but how to go about it? There are some in
> the parish I know, they do not know about me, they would have a
> lot to offer in many ways in parish work, and community work . . .

> Yes. I am finding them when they come for help. *Lots* in the
> priesthood but it's always a hidden and furtive grouping. Oh to be
> open and accepted!

> The more people who are out in the local Christian community the
> better but I do feel that this is a personal choice. I totally disagree

with the practice of 'outing' people. My sexuality is not something I hide. Nor do I deny it if asked but at the same time I haven't got up in the pulpit and announced it to the parishioners.

Possibly, I'm not sure because what I want is people to just accept us as we are and not be seen at all as something special or in need of special attention.

Catholics coming to terms with their sexuality would, of course, benefit from being able to stand up and be counted. The danger for a priest doing so is not just problems with superiors but becoming a 'one issue' person, being a gay priest rather than a priest who happens to be gay.

In principle yes, in practice I have my doubts as to the validity of this question. Being an out gay person has its own problems, particularly with regard to the RC Church in which out gay laity would be subject to a considerable amount of misunderstanding and rejection and gay clergy would be the objects of I think a great amount of consternation not to say rejection in the communities to which they are supposed to minister. So although as I said a moment ago, in principle yes, in practice I have my doubts as to whether more out gay people in the local Church community constitutes a real hope.

David found the witness of 'out' gay clergymen in the Church of England and his contact with gay men through hospice work personally encouraging. Whilst not wanting to be defined as a priest purely in terms of their sexuality nor wishing to be seen as pastors only to gay and lesbian people, it seems that a substantial number of the gay priests at least yearn for the support and friendship of other gay and lesbian people, particularly in their own parish situation. It is the invisibility of lesbian and gay people in our society, an invisibility caused by fear of rejection, that leaves so many feeling isolated. This isolation can be hard to bear in Christian communities where talk of love and acceptance and care is common but often does not extend to non-heterosexuals. For a gay priest the isolation that often accompanies the office can be compounded and sharpened by the feeling that he is the only 'one' in his parish. The one priest who had told some parishioners found them an enormous support.

Towards the end of *Pastores Dabo Vobis* the Pope calls upon the whole

Church to support their priests because priests and laity struggle with the same problems, tensions and pain. But the Vatican's teaching on homosexuality conspires with the homophobia of society in general to keep gay and lesbian people apart by making the risks too great. Gay clergy need gay and lesbian laity and vice versa. Someone has to take the risk.

Undermining the pedestal
The joy and pain of gay priests

In his survey of gay priests in the United States of America James
Wolf discovered that there were significant differences between
gay and non-gay priests in terms of what they liked or disliked
about their lives. Although both groups valued administering the
sacraments extremely highly and enjoyed the respect they received
as a result of their office, non-gay clergy enjoyed administrative
work and the spiritual security of being a priest much more than
gay clergy. On the other hand gay clergy valued developing
friendships, engaging in efforts of social reform and intellectual
and creative activities much more than their non-gay brothers
(*Gay Priests*, pp. 22–5). These broad preferences are also reflected
in our priests' responses to the question 'What do you most and
least like about being a priest?' Among the likes listed were the
following:

> Celebrating the eucharist, meeting and coming to know people,
> helping them sometimes or seeing them sort themselves out, and
> in the pastoral context being and seeing others be 'themselves' —
> in other words, lowering all the defences that human life imposes
> and being exposed to each other — and this being an opportunity
> for growth and deep experiences.

> I would judge that I am fairly 'good with people' and enjoy the
> human relationship side of the priesthood. I have done seven years
> in parish work since finishing my stint in seminary work. Probably
> it is the pastoral side of life that I find most satisfying.

> Just being a priest, my work in our schools, especially our primary
> school, able to help people with the sacraments, and share with

them in the traumas, joys and sorrows. Sharing with them in the Mass.

Being close to people in the deepest way possible and bringing Jesus to bear to make them free from guilt and self-hatred.

The opportunity to walk with others on their journey through life. Sharing with them their joys and sorrows, their success and failure. Also helping others to appreciate the tremendous love God their creator has for them, encouraging people to see that they are created out of love and that they are valued as unique individuals.

I enjoy being a priest, especially my contact with other people, and the insights into life which I am privileged that they share with me. Birth, life and death are continually being presented to me, and this enriches me as a person. I enjoy the liturgy, and this gives me great strength.

My ministry to people and the forming of community.

The satisfaction and fulfilment I get from facilitating people's greater understanding and awareness of themselves, their community, their needs and potential. Healing people and inviting them into the depths of their being and them finding the strength to be fully alive to the world around.

Its unique position. I don't mean position in the sense of privilege but as being all things to all ... Even when you fail. Sense of trust people have in you — honesty, openness.

Celebrating the eucharist and other sacraments ranks highly in the aspects of priesthood most appreciated by gay priests but this is always within the context of their ministry to the people they serve. They describe the good things about their ministry in very person-centred terms. It is being able to be alongside people in their journey through life that seems to bring these men most satisfaction. Several priests specify that it is, in Simon's words, 'the empowering and enabling' of people that gives them particular pleasure, helping them to heal, to learn to love themselves as God loves them and free themselves from guilt and self-hatred. As people who have experienced self-hatred, guilt, rejection, and loneliness on the grounds of their sexuality, these priests seem to be acutely aware of such suffering in others and the need to combat it by building a loving, welcoming community. It is through their humanity and experience as gay men that they reach out to and minister to others. Pope John Paul should be proud of them for they fit his model of priesthood perfectly, except for their sexuality.

In examining the dislikes of priests Wolf once again discovered marked differences between gay and non-gay priests. The biggest difference concerned leading a celibate life: 63 per cent of gay clergy had problems in this area compared to only 11 per cent of priests in general. Gay clergy also felt the loneliness of priesthood more than other priests, had more problems with the authority structures of the Church and their superiors and the relevance of their own work (Wolf, *Gay Priests*, p. 26). Although a number of our respondents had acknowledged celibacy to be a difficulty in other parts of their questionnaire, only two mentioned it explicitly here as one of the things they disliked about being a priest. However, loneliness and problems with Church teaching were among the dislikes listed.

Just being tied down to timetables and routines every day. But I don't think about it, because who isn't?

Not being able to really talk about human sexuality in depth, because I would need to talk about homosexuality and the community would not like this I am sure.

Being the recipient of the usual stereotypes which people have of a priest. Together with this there is a deal of isolation from people which is not easy to handle.

Being part of a Church which can be so unkind and unthinking about a number of issues including homosexuality and third world issues and hurting minority groups.

I am often expected to be a certain kind of person. The pressure to conform and the desire by many people to put you on a pedestal. Above all I hate to spend my life without another person to share my journey within a one to one committed relationship.

The artificiality of the clerical gatherings which one has to attend very often and the many rules and regulations that make it difficult to help people in bad marriage situations or gay relationships or whatever, together with the problems of sharing with other Christians at every level, especially the eucharist.

Having to be so circumspect about my sexuality and being seen to represent oppressive doctrines.

Applying the law in hard cases.

Involvement with Catholic school system. Dealing with 'pious' old women. Failure of others in the parish to play their part. False role cast by religious old traditional Catholics.

Several mention what Simon calls the 'pedestal syndrome', de-humanizing the priest and investing him with expectations and stereotypes which he cannot or does not want to live up to. Representing a Church which often seems hard, uncaring and uncompassionate on sexual matters must be a particular burden to a gay priest. The implicitly enforced silence and invisibility imposed upon them as gay men also takes its toll and reinforces loneliness and isolation as do the attitudes of fellow clergy. The seminarians' expectations of what they would like or dislike about priesthood makes interesting reading. Thomas looks forward to 'being loved and affirmed by so many', as he had been during his time as a lay pastoral assistant. One can only hope that he finds such affirmation; the gay priests in our survey had not found such universal affirma-tion. Indeed, he indicates that he knows his hopes will not be completely realized because his prospective dislikes are 'being dis-tanced by others, not being treated as a human person'. Vernon looks forward to experiencing Christ's love and liberation in his own life and then bringing it to others. He does not look forward to having to be judged purely on his ability to conform himself to the expectations of the institutional Church.

The gay priests who responded to the questionnaire are intensely human men, they have little time for the trappings and status of being a priest and find the isolation and idealization of the office hard to bear. They understand the Gospel and their ministry in terms of relationships and use the language of sharing, liberation and healing a great deal. The parts of their ministry that bring them close to people are the parts they enjoy most, whilst they dislike those parts which push them apart from people. Their sexuality, and experience of rejection by Church and society because of it, undoubtedly contributes to their person-centred ministry. These priests come across as ideal priests according to the vision of the Second Vatican Council, working with the laity, understanding their ministry in terms of the priest as pastor rather than sacerdotal figure. In a study of the characteristics people most value in their priests the following were among the most valued: personal integrity; personal, lived religion; competence and a sense of responsibility; an empathetic counsellor (Sipe, *A Secret World*, p. 279). The priests and seminarians in our study seem to embody these ideals. The Church should be proud of them.

'You are not alone'
Advice to future gay priests

The final question asked of the priests and seminarians was what advice the respondent would give to gay men considering the priesthood. Not one of the respondents suggested that the priesthood should be avoided by gay men, although most recommended that careful thought should be given before a commitment to the priesthood is made because 'there is a costly price to be paid' in terms of celibacy and stress connected with sexuality.

Think it through very carefully and see if you can a) remain celibate, b) avoid a close personal relationship, c) discuss it with other priests or a spiritual adviser.

The need to find a trustworthy person to talk to — a spiritual director or soul friend — is one emphasized by many of the priests. Connected with this is the need to be honest with oneself about sexuality. The need for this honest acceptance of one's sexual orientation is emphasized by all the respondents.

Accept yourself as you are. Love yourself in all that you are — your person, your body.

Be close to God, and freely speak to Him about your gayness. Maybe pray to Christ in words like 'You know me, I'm gay ... ; some say your friend, John was gay; I hope he was because your love for him was so clear, and that takes away any doubts I have of your love for me.' Talk to your spiritual director, *in confession*, if you want to, but be firmly founded in Christ first, so that if he is not able to appreciate you or what you say, you already have the greater spiritual bedrock.

God does seem to like choosing gays to be priests. This must say something. An awareness of one's sexuality is important for all students. Celibacy is the question not the orientation.

Be as honest as you feel you can be!

Honesty with oneself is essential but what about with others? Brian found his experience of being 'outed' at seminary 'liberating', but a priest who used to be on the staff of a seminary advises:

Having been in seminary work I know very well the scenarios. The cynical bit of me would advise a gay student to keep it dark before ordination, otherwise there is a definite possibility of being 'thrown out'. It is a brave man who owns his homosexuality in seminary and I would admire his courage. Whether the seminary staff or his bishop would leave it at that is another matter.

Another priest recommends choosing an environment where honesty with others will be possible:

Try and find a bishop or religious congregation that welcomes you as a gay person. Be honest with yourself and with others and never apologize for the fact that you are gay. Give thanks to God each day for the gift of your sexuality and don't keep that gift to yourself.

But another warns:

Be careful. Keep your gay contacts with the respectable gay scene but be discreet. Don't respond to authorities in such a way as to satisfy their homophobic worries, i.e. be honest but don't answer prying unnecessary questions. Belong to LGCM.

The importance of accepting gay sexuality as a gift is reflected in the majority of replies.

Gayness *can* be a gift from God. It may be that a gay is especially chosen: he has gifts of sensitivity that others do not. But be aware of the pain — isolation within himself and not having friends, i.e. the Cross.

My advice to any gay student to the priesthood is to 'hang in there'. You have something very precious to offer the Church in being a loving and caring person. The Church needs you to give another facet of the person of God, and if things are going to change for the better, then you are needed to help things change. Most of all, YOU ARE NOT ALONE.

Don't let this be a problem. Accept yourself as you are and as God loves you and know that your ministry will be enhanced by your own sufferings and problems in this area.

However two priests remind potential students that being gay does not make them superior or absolve them from following the rules.

Don't think being gay makes you special. That's the problem, we do make being gay a big deal.

Being gay does not mean promiscuous. Remember that many of your straight colleagues would, on some nights, be wishing they were in another's bed, and be fighting to control this. A gay priest can do marvellous work. But if he has not acquired self-control, the help and support he might give could easily turn into something else. The self-control your straight friends must learn will enable them to work with some of 'the ravishing blondes' who come their way; it will be the same for you with some of the young men you meet.

Three priests offer advice to those students who find themselves falling in love or faced with the possibility of a sexual relationship.

Don't be ashamed if you break the rules, they are human-made and have little to do with being a good priest and don't let guilt feelings ruin your ministry. If you find a lover and friend who helps you to be more of your true self accept it as a blessing from God but be careful about just using people as 'one-night stands' because you are afraid to enter into a long-term commitment.

Do not be afraid of falling in love. Recognize beauty wherever you may find it, savour it but try not to possess it. Remember that genital activity is overrated and can never in its all satisfy your longing for true love and intimacy.

Simon warns of the tensions that a sexual relationship will cause in a priest's life.

The seminarians who took part in the survey shared the priests' conviction that gayness is not an obstacle to ordination and indeed should be regarded as a gift that can be brought to the vocation for the gift of the whole Church. One of them sums up the feelings of both priests and seminarians in one sentence: 'Be true to yourself, but be careful who you talk to'.

The priests were also asked whether there was anything they knew now about sexuality and priesthood that they wish they had known before ordination. Three priests wondered whether they would have presented themselves for ordination if they had come to terms with their sexuality earlier.

It is all a matter of 'ifs' and guessing, but if I had been able to accept my homosexuality fully as a young man I wonder if I would have gone on to ordination. Maybe yes, maybe no. But I started trying my vocation thirty years ago and it was a different world then.

Only one priest suggested that if he had known the difficulties and pain involved in being a gay priest he would not have been ordained. Others just wished that they had been better prepared.

Yes — the difficulty of being gay in an anti-gay organization. I think it will change for priests also in 100 years time — but now, Oh the pain.

Yes, the difficulties involved in living a life of celibacy. I have made a commitment to ministry but I don't accept celibacy as essential or desirable.

I wish I had known that a relationship was a real possibility within the priesthood.

I wish I'd known before I was ordained that it was possible to be more open with other gay students in the seminary and so avoid the heavy psychological toll which making myself pass as straight to myself, as well as to others, took on me. On the other hand, given the presence of homophobia among some of the higher clergy and so presumably among at least some of those responsible for training the clergy I would reiterate, with regret, what I said earlier about the only sure-fire safe way to get through the seminary if you're gay is to go back in the closet and lock the door on the inside. Some gay priests would dispute this and I understand their reason for doing so on the grounds that more openness between students and indeed between staff and students in the seminary about homosexuality would be very desirable. However, I am happier standing by what I said in the interests of common prudence and making sure one gets through the seminary, so sadly I must stand by that, although I realize that that is not constructive advice to a student for the priesthood.

Just how 'non simpatico' most priests are!

Several priests echoed Simon in wishing they had had more contact with the gay community as this would have made them feel less isolated and abnormal and would also have given them support and hope for the future.

I wish I had been more actively involved in the gay community as a student as I didn't realize then what potential we had for change in the Church and what beautiful people we are.

To sum up, the advice to gay men thinking of entering the seminary or religious order is: know and accept yourself; recognize your sexuality as a gift; always be honest with yourself; ideally find an institution which allows you to be out and is prepared to acknowledge your sexuality in your formation; find a trustworthy spiritual director to whom you can be out; think very carefully about the demands of celibacy; find support within the gay community whilst being careful about who you talk to; face the fact that your sexuality will cause you difficulty in the Church.

There is a wealth of wisdom here, acquired through a great deal of personal pain and trauma, which could ease the suffering of future generations of gay clergy and seminarians. But once again the point must be made that for the Church to provide the best possible formation for its gay clergy it first has to acknowledge that they exist and that they can make as good priests and religious as heterosexual men. This book testifies to the fact that some gay men are chosen to be ordained and serve the Church through the whole of their persons, of which their sexuality is a very significant part. Some parts of the Church are beginning to recognize and appreciate the gift of gay pastors. Since the Church always changes from the bottom up, this is a good sign but these men deserve the recognition and support of their superiors and bishops and of the Vatican. In his study of celibacy Richard Sipe has argued that 'in the Roman Catholic Church, the most logical place for sexuality to be re-evaluated and the basis of a theology of sex to be formulated is within the structure of its celibate clergy' ('Sex and Celibacy', *The Tablet*, 9 May 1992).

Similarly, I believe that the Vatican's reassessment of homosexuality will begin when it is forced to recognize its presence in the Church's own faithful, hard-working and well-balanced clergy. Many gay and lesbian people greatly fear coming out to their families because they have never heard anything but negative comments on homosexuality from their parents, siblings and so on. But many are surprised by how quickly their family's attitude to homosexuality changes once they realize that one of their own is gay or lesbian. Preconceived notions of lesbian and gay people can dissolve before the reality of the person they know and love. I hope that the same process might occur in the Church family if it faces the reality of gay priests who are obviously not disordered or dangerous. I hope that by giving gay priests in Britain a forum through which to tell their stories this book will make a modest contribution to this process.

The way forward
Recommendations

The recurrent theme of this book has been that the Roman Catholic Church needs to face the reality of gay priests. God seems to be choosing gay men to serve in the ordained ministry and no amount of screening or weeding out or anti-homosexual teaching appears to prevent gay men fulfilling their vocation, although they experience a great deal of pain in the process from having to conceal or deny their sexuality. It could be argued that the attitude to gay priests will not change until the Church's teaching on homosexuality changes but, as I have already mentioned, I believe that it is gay priests who could motivate a change in the Vatican's assessment of homosexuality. For this to happen gay clergy have to become visible within the Church, their voice has to be heard, their witness to the fact that gay people are not necessarily disordered must be seen. Bishops, superiors and rectors must therefore create safe space for gay students and gay priests to reflect upon their own experience and forums where dialogue between these men and their superiors can take place. The gay men will need to be loved into speech. They will need to be assured that they can confide in their superiors without adverse results. They will need to feel cherished and valued as gay men, and it will take a long time to build up enough trust for that to happen. The following recommendations are offered to bishops, superiors and seminary rectors who wish to take the first steps along that road. Considering the present climate in the Catholic Church, it is a brave bishop or man in authority who will face the reality of gay clergy and seek to minister to them and learn from them. Ultimately, however, their loyalty is not to the Congregation for the Doctrine of Faith but to the one who recognized God in the religious and social outcasts of his day — the ones who could never have become Jewish priests — and who promised 'the truth will make you free' (John 8:32).

Recommendations

1. Theologians should continue to study homosexuality, drawing upon the best and latest research undertaken by the human sciences, ideally without censure for not 'toeing the party line', but continuing even if censured.

2. Bishops, superiors and seminary rectors should keep themselves up to date on the subject.

3. Continuing education on the subject should be offered to diocesan personnel, members of religious orders and seminary tutors. This education should be informed by the realities of people's lives rather than the abstractions of moral theology.

4. Each diocese or religious order should consider setting up an independent and confidential counselling service for gay clergy.

5. The setting up of support groups for gay clergy should be allowed and encouraged with the aim of fostering personal growth rather than ecclesiastical control.

6. The laity need to be re-educated on the nature of priesthood and encouraged to take responsibility for the well-being of their pastors.

7. The Church needs to demonstrate genuine pastoral care for all gay and lesbian people. And it must not be ashamed of being seen to do so.

8. Bishops, religious orders and seminaries should construct and publish a policy on gay candidates, honestly stating the criteria for acceptance or rejection. The ego-dystonic criterion proposed in some places should be clearly rejected as against the spirit of *Pastores Dabo Vobis* and dangerous to the mental health of individual priests and to the pastoral care they are called to offer to others.

9. Seminaries need to review the handling of the issue of homosexuality, acknowledging the existence of gay priests and seminarians. In particular, in educating students for celibacy, the unique concerns of gay men need to be addressed without gay candidates being sub-

jected to unfair treatment or prejudice. Seminaries should offer gay candidates personal witness from gay priests.

10. In their 1979 pastoral guidelines on the care of homosexual people the Catholic Social Welfare Commission of the bishops of England and Wales noted that:

> It is the role of the pastor to offer encouragement and support. Many good people who are homosexual are constantly struggling against the demands of their condition and they must not be allowed to despair. It is unworthy of a pastor to offer only superficial advice for such an intractable problem.

> Pastors can be especially helpful in the 'coming out' process ... The pastor seems to be an obvious person with whom to share these confidences and his own response must be sensitive and sympathetic.

Perhaps the very existence of this book will encourage those who have pastoral care of clergy to stop and reflect whether they are offering that kind of pastoral care to their gay brothers in Christ. For the sake of all those men suffering because they have been chosen to be Catholic, gay and ordained, I hope so.

Appendix: The questionnaire

This is the questionnaire used in the survey upon which this book is based.

LESBIAN AND GAY CHRISTIAN MOVEMENT — ROMAN CATHOLIC CAUCUS

We would like to enlist your help with a short book we are preparing on gay Catholic priests. The aim is to use anonymous testimonies and to reflect the actual experience of British Catholic priests in a way that will be helpful to other gay priests, to priests who are having problems with their sexuality, and to students for the priesthood.

Below are some questions which you might like to take as a starting point. Please write your answers to these or anything else you feel is appropriate on the reverse of these sheets.

---

1. Are you happy to be gay?

2. What is your view of the Church's teaching on homosexuality?
   2a. How did you react to the 1986 'Letter on the Pastoral Care of Homosexual Persons'?
   2b. Did it change your behaviour and attitudes in any way?

3. Did you know you were gay before you began your training?
   3a. What effect did your time at seminary have on your under-

standing and acceptance of your sexuality?

3b. Was the issue of homosexuality among the clergy dealt with at seminary? If so, how?

4. How comfortable are you with the discipline of celibacy?

4a. If you are sexually active does this have any effect on your wider ministry as a priest? Do you feel guilty about this?

4b. If you are *not* sexually active does this have any effect on your wider ministry as a priest?

4c. What helps you to remain celibate?

5. Does your being gay affect your relationship with other clergy?

6. What support networks do you find helpful?

6a. Does your bishop/superior know that you are gay?

6b. As a gay priest do you think you can count on the support of your bishop/superior?

7. Are you involved with 'Justice and Peace' work as part of your ministry?

Do you think that the Church should be concerned with the rights of lesbian and gay people as a justice issue or are you more comfortable with homosexuality being seen as a moral issue?

8. What do you like most about being a priest?

9. What do you like least about being a priest?

10. Are you involved with the 'out' gay community at all?

11. Do you think it would be helpful to you/other gay or lesbian Catholics if there were more 'out' gay people in the local Church community?

12. Have you had any particularly positive or negative experiences in the Church as a result of your sexuality?

13. Is there anything you know now that you wish you'd known before you were ordained?

14. What advice would you give to a gay student for the priesthood?

Thank you for your help. I assure you that all testimonies will be completely anonymous. In the final published version any names, places and dates will be removed. You do not have to identify yourself when replying. Please pass a copy of these questions to any other gay priests who may be interested in participating in this survey.

Bibliography

John Boswell, *Christianity, Social Tolerance, and Homosexuality: Gay People in Western Europe from the Beginning of the Christian Era to the Fourteenth Century* (University of Chicago Press, Chicago, 1980).

Catholic Social Welfare Commission, *An Introduction to the Pastoral Care of Homosexual People* (Catholic Information Services, Abbots Langley, 1979; available from LGCM, Oxford House, Derbyshire Street, London E2 6HG).

Congregation for the Doctrine of Faith, *Declaration on Certain Questions Concerning Sexual Ethics* (Rome, 1975).

Congregation for the Doctrine of Faith, *Letter to the Bishops of the Catholic Church on the Pastoral Care of Homosexual Persons* (Rome, 1986).

Congregation for the Doctrine of Faith, *Some Considerations Concerning the Catholic Response to Legislative Proposals on the Non-Discrimination of Homosexual Persons* (Rome, 1992).

Congregation for Institutes of Consecrated Life and Societies of Apostolic Life, *Directives on Formation in Religious Institutes* (Rome, 1990).

Ben Fletcher, *Clergy Under Stress: A Study of Homosexual and Heterosexual Clergy in the Church of England* (Mowbray, London, 1990).

Jeannine Gramick, *Homosexuality in the Priesthood and the Religious Life* (Crossroad, New York, 1989).

Jeannine Gramick and Pat Furey, *The Vatican and Homosexuality: Reactions to the 'Letter to the Bishops of the Catholic Church on the Pastoral Care of Homosexual Persons'* (Crossroad, New York, 1988).

Adrian Hastings, *Modern Catholicism: Vatican II and After* (SPCK,

London, 1991).

John Paul II, *Pastores Dabo Vobis: Apostolic Exhortation of His Holiness John Paul II on the Formation of Priests* (Rome, 1992).

John J. McNeill, *The Church and the Homosexual* (3rd edition, Beacon Press, Boston, 1988).

Gareth Moore, *The Body in Context: Sex and Catholicism* (SCM, London, 1992).

Robert Nugent, *A Challenge to Love: Gay and Lesbian Catholics in the Church* (Crossroad, New York, 1989).

Robert Nugent and Jeannine Gramick, *Building Bridges: Gay and Lesbian Reality and the Catholic Church* (Twenty-Third Publications, Connecticut, 1992).

Tony Philpot, *Brothers in Christ: A Call to Fraternity in the Diocesan Priesthood* (Kevin Mayhew, Bury St Edmunds, 1991).

A. W. Richard Sipe, *A Secret World: Sexuality and the Search for Celibacy* (Brunner/Mazel, New York, 1990).

James Wolf, *Gay Priests* (Harper and Row, San Francisco, 1989).

This book is based upon a project set up by the Roman Catholic Caucus of the Lesbian and Gay Christian Movement, Oxford House, Derbyshire Street, London E2 6HG (tel: 071–739 1249).